IOLS '91
Integrated Online Library Systems

PROCEEDINGS—1991

New York, May 8-9, 1991

Sponsored by
Learned Information, Inc.

Compiled by
David C. Genaway
Youngstown State University and
Genaway & Associates, Inc.

Learned Information, Inc.
Medford, NJ

IOLS '91
Proceedings of the Sixth National Conference on Integrated Online Library Systems

New York, May 8-9, 1991

PROGRAM CHAIRMAN
David C. Genaway
Youngstown State University

MEETING ORGANIZER
Thomas H. Hogan
Learned Information, Inc.

ORGANIZING/REVIEWING COMMITTEE

Brian Alley	Sangamon State University
Ching-chih Chen	Simmons College
Lynn Heer	NASA STAC
Judy McQueen	Library Consultant
Donald E. Riggs	University of Michigan

Price: $30.00
Order from: Learned Information, Inc.
143 Old Marlton Pike
Medford, NJ 08055

Cover Design: Mary McDonnell

ISBN: 0-938734-52-0
© 1991 by Learned Information, Inc., Medford, New Jersey.
All rights reserved.

PREFACE

IOLS '91, the sixth national conference on Integrated Online Library Systems, met on May 8 and 9 in New York City in conjunction with the National Online Meeting sponsored by Learned Information, Inc.

If there is a theme for IOLS '91, it is "Solutions": solutions to systems, storage, access, staff, and communications problems. There is a growing concern for integrating CD-ROMs and other indexes into online catalogs as reflected in the several papers regarding the next generation of catalogs. Communications, linkage and document delivery are also evident. Interest in system selection, acquisition, migration, and satisfaction remains high. Of increasing concern is personnel management, particularly in relation to integration of library and computer staff.

These proceedings were compiled by David C. Genaway, Program Chair, under the general organization of Thomas Hogan, Meeting Organizer. Much of the credit for the production of the proceedings goes to Carol Nixon, who worked directly with contributors in seeing that production schedules were met. The Program/Review Committee consisting of Brian Alley, Sangamon State University, Ching-chih Chen, Simmons College, Lynn Heer, NASA STAC, Judy McQueen, Library Consultant, and Donald E. Riggs, University of Michigan deserve special recognition for their time and energy involved in evaluating and selecting contributed papers. Most of them also served as chairs of the various sessions.

TABLE OF CONTENTS

LIS: An Electronic Library for the Future
Naomi C. Broering 1

Methodology for Determining Database Integrity for Your Newly Loaded Database: Error Detection and Resolution
Cass Brush 11

The Unseen Power Behind the Integrated System: A Comparison of Various Operating Systems
Mary H. Casey 19

Integrating External Files into an Online Catalog: Comparative Search Strategies
Kellian D. Clink 25

The Public Services Librarian as System Administrator
Gregory A. Crawford 33

One ALD for Both Reader and Technical Services: A New Organizational Model for Administration
Frieda M. Davison 39

Library Field Trials and the Solution to Problems of Information Retrieval in the Large
Horace Dediu and S.C. Chang 45

DLS MARC-UP: Upgrading a Centralized Online Bibliographic Database
Sandra R. Donahue 53

Educational Constructs for Computer and Library Science Personnel
Charles D. Hurt 59

System Migration: Bettering Tomorrow Today
William Jacob 65

Farewell to Technocracy: A Public Service Manifesto for the Online Catalog
Lee Jaffe 73

HyperRef: An Expert System for the Reference Desk
Corinne Jörgensen and Peter Jörgensen 75

Choices: Collection Management Issues of the IOLS
George S. Machovec, Dennis R. Brunning, and Joyce Plaza 83

Selection and Adaptation of Library Systems in a Changing Environment
Sharon B. Mehl 93

Library and Computing Staff: Learning from One Another
Ray E. Metz 97

Beyond Subject Access: The Next Generation of OPAC Software
Mary Micco and Thomas Basista 103

Library Automation and the Advent of the Knowledge Network
Todd Miller 113

CD-ROM as Backup for Rockwell International's RTIS/TECHLIB System
Martha T. Mori 119

Satisfaction and Dissatisfaction with IOLS Hardware
Lester J. Pourciau 123

Academic Libraries and Academic Computer Centers: United We Stand; Divided We Fall
Pal V. Rao 131

Library Networking in Vermont: An Analysis of Usage Patterns and Cost-effectiveness
Jeffrey R. Rehbach 137

UNIX on the Library Scene
Kathleen Robertson 141

Let's Make a Deal: Donor-driven Library Systems in a Non-profit Institution
Carol J. Snyder 145

Beyond the Online Catalog: Current Developments and Future Directions of New England Library Automation
Diane R. Tebbetts 149

The Power of Library Administrators Meets the Power of Technology
Kieth C. Wright 157

Titles of Papers Presented at the Meeting for Which Text Does Not Appear in the Proceedings 169

Index 171

IOLS '91
Integrated Online Library Systems

PROCEEDINGS—1991

LIS: AN ELECTRONIC LIBRARY FOR THE FUTURE

Naomi C. Broering, Georgetown University

Keywords: Integrated Online Library System, miniMEDLINE, Current Contents, BIOETHICSLINE, IAIMS, Document Delivery

Abstract: A hallmark of the Georgetown University Library Information System is the design flexibility that allows for growth and expansion using a modular approach. The LIS, an integrated online library system developed in 1981, includes all basic library functions such as circulation, catalog and cataloging utilities, acquisitions and serials modules. In 1982, the miniMEDLINE SYSTEM, a bibliographic subset based on the NLM MEDLINE file was developed. Special features added from 1985 to 1990 include ALERTS/CURRENT CONTENTS, BIOETHICSLINE, Electronic News, a Multiple Library System (MLS) and Reserve Room. A Document Delivery system that offers photocopy, mail and fax options is being tested for immediate release. New products targeted for the future are full-text and E-Mail modules. Each of the LIS modules has report generators for library statistical data. The system has network capabilities beyond the library walls i.e., to the medical center, community, vendors and other campuses.

During the past decade the LIS has emerged into a comprehensive integrated system that handles more than typical library functions. Its special features are in-house bibliographic databases and access to BRS full text and other systems. The LIS also interfaces to a Knowledge Network of information, diagnostic and clinical databases available as part of the Integrated Academic Information Management System (IAIMS) project supported by the NLM. The IAIMS project includes a Macintosh interface which is an icon based prototype designed to facilitate system use. The LIS evolutionary process includes plans for an intelligent, graphic/window/image based system and a full-text transmission system. The LIS continues its pioneering efforts on the forefront of library automation. It is entering a new exciting phase with windows of opportunity aimed toward developing a next generation library system.

1. A LIBRARY SYSTEM FOR TOMORROW

Recent advances in information technology offer a library an opportunity to provide services beyond its walls, beyond its traditional service domain, and essentially, beyond anything previously imagined. The "trick" for the librarian seeking a library system today, is to determine which one of the many choices available in the marketplace offers innovative features that enhances the role of the library in the institution. Which system can make it a truly electronic library for the future? A few years ago, librarians were satisfied with stand-alone systems such as circulation or serials. The trend in the last five years, has been to acquire integrated library systems with basic functions such as an online catalog, cataloging, circulation, serials and acquisitions. Amazingly, some systems do not yet offer all these minimal capabilities; they offer only partially completed systems. However, as libraries march into the 21st century, they need to offer more services to their users.

In the past, some libraries in need of an easy solution that required minimal technical knowledge contracted for turnkey automated systems. This means that implementation of hardware, software, system peripherals and facility preparation was turned-over to a vendor and the library was relieved of installation "headaches". However, this approach does not prepare library staff to become technically competent about computer systems. This approach is acceptable, if professional development is not a goal of the library, and if the library is confident that the turnkey vendor will offer a broad array of modules in the future. Usually turnkey packages are limited in scope, inflexible, awkward to network and committed to specific brands of hardware and peripherals to be acquired only through the vendor. Watch out for this, because it means you are boxed into a "take it-or-leave-it situation" at a set price, which is not usually a bargain. Turnkey vendors rarely invest in R&D of new technical approaches, and when new brands and new features become available, the library is locked into a sole source for its system features and equipment.

Libraries that have chosen a more independent, software-only approach are generally free to implement new, innovative services and to add new modules to enhance their role in the institution. Also, because these libraries have taken a liberal approach to providing professional development, their staff are usually more creative and technically competent to add new features to the library's system. The key, then, is to stay flexible and choose a software system that is modular and can offer futuristic features.

In 1983, Jones and Marcum stated, "the focus of integrated systems has been on library systems that manipulate the bibliographic record. This concept must shift to one that involves the integration of many information systems, and with this shift in focus comes a new perspective to the role of the library." (1) We are at that point now; the issue is not to merely automate, but to make an important strategic move to elevate the library through new electronic services. Libraries automating for the first time and those acquiring second systems have more choices today. These libraries are in an excellent position to look for a software system that offers more than just the "basic package". They would be wise to find one with the ability to network and integrate new modules. These libraries should position themselves to move into the next generation of library systems.

To illustrate what I mean about the next generation of integrated systems, I will describe how the Georgetown University Library Information System (LIS) has grown over the past ten years and become key to the Integrated Academic Information Management System (IAIMS), project, an National Library of Medicine (NLM) grant initiative. Our medical center library has emerged, through IAIMS, as a focal point for integration of information flow in the medical center. The medical library's databases are an essential part of information systems accessed through the institution's IAIMS Knowledge Network. (2) The purpose of the Knowledge Network is to transmit biomedical information from various sources to users at the place and time it is needed. It is part of "tomorrow's environment" where integration of information occurs at the system level, and the multiplicity of sources are transparent to users. We believe this approach to information management is applicable to other libraries and is already evident in the corporate sector.

2. LIS: IS A STEPPING STONE TO THE FUTURE

"Bringing the library to the user" was the rationale for the library automation project launched in 1980 by the Dahlgren Memorial Library at the Georgetown University Medical Center. A decision was made to design an integrated library information system and maintain library records in one coordinated computer system. By 1981, version 1.0 of the Georgetown University (TM) Library Information System (LIS) was completed. The components designed in LIS handled the basic functions normally included in an integrated system (cataloging, circulation, acquisitions, serials). By 1982, the LIS included additional features, beyond the basic functions, such as in-house bibliographic databases, networking, and word processing report generators. The miniMEDLINE SYSTEM (TM), a self-service bibliographic module which allows users to execute searches of a portion of the NLM's MEDLINE file, was the first in-house database available in the library system. (3)

Today, the latest LIS version is 4.3, a radically enhanced and expanded system with a multitude of added capabilities for library users. LIS includes a series of value added features: the ALERTS(TM)/CURRENT CONTENTS(R) Search System, BIOETHICSLINE, Document Delivery, Reserves and a Multiple Library Version. In addition, as part of the IAIMS project, other databases, besides the bibliographic systems, include information, diagnostic, research and gateway systems. We now have a family of databases joined together to form a Knowledge Network of medical decision support systems for Georgetown users. These varied systems interface to the LIS in a single access menu through BioSYNTHESIS a retrieval system (see menu levels below).

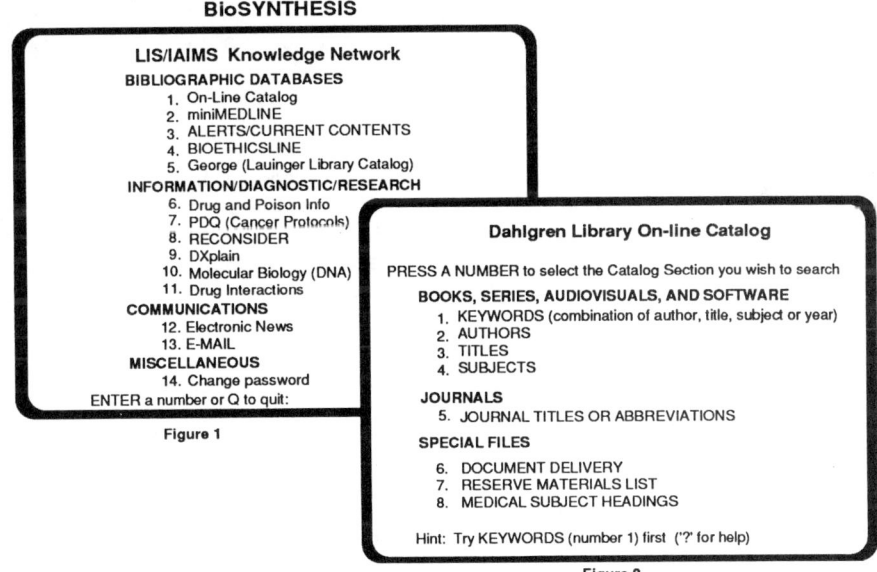

Figure 1

Figure 2

3. LIS UPDATE

The last time LIS was reported in the literature, (4,5,6) the system was operating under version 3.0, but since then, many new components have been added which are highlighted in this paper. One of the most significant additions to LIS was the Multiple Library System (MLS); it has a unique approach for a main library to add branches or other institutional libraries to its central computer system. Overall, the features which LIS users favor have been maintained; it is menu driven with one entry point and clean screen displays (figure 2). In the Online Catalog, the miniMEDLINE SYSTEM, ALERTS/CURRENT

CONTENTS and BIOETHICSLINE users access information consistently through two steps: 1) to enter their search term(s), and 2) to display or print selected references.

3.1 The Online Public Access Catalog and MARC Utilities

The catalog contains records of the library's holdings, including books, journals, and audiovisuals. It provides users with a dictionary as well as a divided catalog for accessing holding information. The search points - which include keyword (Boolean AND), Author, Title, and Subject (Boolean OR) - have been enhanced extensively. There are still three levels of record display, but users have more search capabilities. The first two are an abbreviated display and a full display that replicates the card catalog and contains the call number as well as the circulation status and location of the item. The third is a detailed MARC record display used primarily by the cataloger for maintenance of the master bibliographic file. MARC records enter the system via magtape, online transfer from OCLC, or direct keyboard input. The record is then modified as needed and stored in LIS. The CD-ROM OPAC replaced a microfilm backup catalog.

3.2 Circulation

All standard circulation functions such as check-in, checkout, renewals, holds, overdue, fine notices, patron notices, inquiry and reports have been expanded. The major files are comprised of patron and item files (books, journals, or audiovisuals) with barcode cross reference. Management reports on patron use and extensive statistical gathering are included. An IBM PC based backup circulation system has been added to collect circulation-transaction data if the main system is down.

3.3 Acquisitions

This component is totally integrated with LIS; it interfaces with the circulation system for the item file and with the public online catalog so patrons are immediately aware of on-order or in-process items. It also provides a single point for pre-order searching by staff. The acquisitions module contains files for regular and standing orders, vendors, and fiscal transactions. It produces order, claim, cancel, and return forms and provides fiscal reports and statistical data.

3.4 Serials

The serials component is MARC based. It allows the library to maintain journal bibliographic records that follow national standards. There is also a capability to output holdings data for the NLM DOCLINE database. A major advantage of a fully integrated serials control system is that, the instant new issues are received and checked-in, the information is immediately accessible to the public in the online catalog. Other special features of the serials component include subject searching, claiming, binding control, routing, and capabilities to load subscription data from vendor invoice tapes.

3.5 Networking

The networking features allow dial-up to the system from remote sites. Users and local libraries are given access codes. The campus network provides medical center users with automatic access to all the databases.

3.6 Office Management (Word Processing)

The office automation system includes a word processing feature that is used in conjunction with the report generators and for preparing library reports where more than one individual participates in writing the manuscript. LIS help screens are also maintained in the word processor. This allows individual libraries to edit the screens if desired.

4. LIS VALUE ADDED FEATURES

The additional bibliographic and informational databases available with LIS make it one of the most outstanding and unique systems available today. This section includes a brief description of the special value added modules of LIS.

4.1 The miniMEDLINE SYSTEM

This user-friendly bibliographic search system provides access to a subset of the NLM MEDLINE file. It is a collection-oriented, in-house system designed for use by students, residents, researchers, and faculty seeking basic information in the core journal literature held by the library. Today, the database contains over 1,000 journals including citations and abstracts covering the most recent five years. Georgetown subscribes to the NLM MEDLINE tapes and converts the records to the miniMEDLINE format. The file is updated monthly. The enhanced version includes capabilities to search a growing database rapidly, to retrieve abstracts, and to incorporate the annually revised Mesh tapes released by NLM. New capabilities are continually added without disrupting the intuitive approach to searching. Users can still conduct their searches through the established menu with nine options. The miniMEDLINE SYSTEM is clearly the "front runner" in popularity with users. ALERTS/CURRENT CONTENTS is new, only two years. (see figure 3)

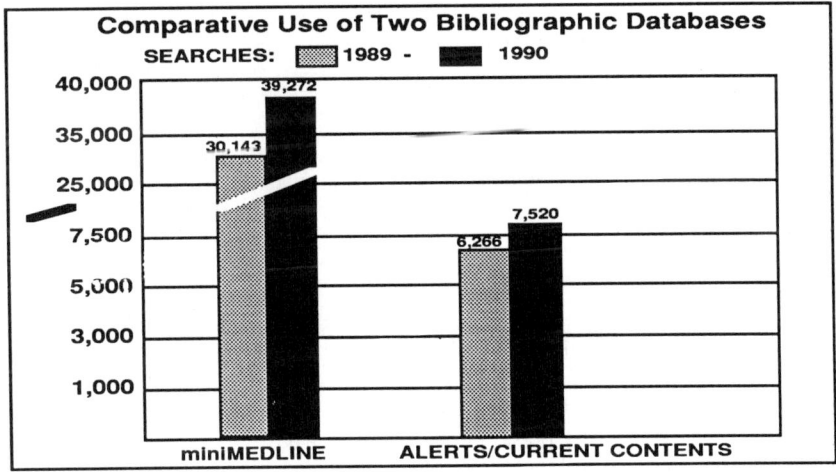

Figure 3

4.2 ALERTS/CURRENT CONTENTS Search System

This component is based on a subset of the Institute for Scientific Information's (ISI) CURRENT CONTENTS database, which contains an index of the latest articles in scientific subjects published in journals. The ALERTS interface software is a user-friendly, self-service bibliographic search system with retrieval routines similar to those of miniMEDLINE, but it has added features. It provides the ability to store a search strategy for use at a later date. Search access is by author, title word, or journal. It displays single or combined sets with Boolean operators and automatically prints lists of references selected by the user. Georgetown uses the five sections of CURRENT CONTENTS: Biology and Environmental Sciences, Chemical and Earth Sciences, Clinical Practice, Life Sciences, and Technology and Applied Science. The system has gained popularity with basic and clinical science researchers of the Medical Center.

4.3 BIOETHICSLINE System

This database, developed at Georgetown in collaboration with the NLM, was recently added to LIS. It supports the growing interest in medical ethics and the surging impact of ethical issues in biotechnology and genetics.

4.4 Multiple Library System (MLS)

The MLS version is popular with large libraries because it enables them to form an affiliated library network to share a computer system. Affiliated libraries selected for inclusion in the network share a master bibliographic file, while maintaining their own patron and item files. With this approach users can easily search the catalog of each affiliated or branch library and also the union catalog of the libraries participating in the network. This module offers prospects for further network features that will be important when NREN becomes a reality.

4.5 Reserve Room

This module includes special capabilities for handling reserve items, such as reprints, which are not included in the master bibliographic file. Patrons may search reserves through the main catalog menu by course name, course number, instructor, author, or title. Reserve lending is handled through the circulation module.

4.6 Document Delivery

This full-service document delivery service, which allows both individual users and other libraries to request loans, photocopies and fax transmissions, has been developed and is being tested. It will be available to LIS libraries in early fall 1991.

4.7 Future LIS Features

A few modules and enhancements, planned in the future, but important to mention are the serial vendor interface to companies such as FAXON, EBSCO, Readmore and Majors, the new updates to OCLC services, a full-text digital imaging transmission system, graphics interface and an E-Mail component.

5. LIS AND THE KNOWLEDGE NETWORK

LIS serves as a hub for IAIMS activities and has inspired development of projects that have led to the Knowledge Network, a family of medical databases. The two systems (LIS and IAIMS) are becoming almost synonymous. The special IAIMS databases, mentioned previously in this paper, harmoniously link to LIS databases. Together they are evolving into a useful, decision-support system for medical center students, researchers, and practitioners seeking information for improved patient care. This feature of being able to add multiple databases and to facilitate multiple database searching is a key element for the electronic library of the future. For example, non-medical libraries can apply the Knowledge Network concept to bring other types of institutional databases to their users.

5.1 BioSYNTHESIS: A Tool for System Integration

BioSYNTHESIS, an intelligent retrieval system, is the tool which interfaces and integrates databases based on disparate computer systems.(7) Design features of BioSYNTHESIS include a mechanism that responds to a user query for bibliographic or factual information by searching the Knowledge Network databases on whatever computers they may reside. The system links heterogeneous computers. Georgetown uses DEC VAX, AT&t 3B2s and SUN 490 minicomputers. Front-end access is through Macintosh, IBM PC computers and intelligent terminals. LIS is written in MUMPS and BioSYNTHESIS is written in C language functioning in UNIX.

5.2 Links to Knowledge Network Databases

The library has assumed responsibility for providing a body of knowledge resources to medical center users that enhance and support medical decision making. In addition to bibliographic systems, we have added informational, research and diagnostic systems, which are accessed from the single menu cited previously. They are as follows:

Information Databases
- **The MicroMedex System,** Drug and Poison sections which include education and Martindale's Pharmacopoeia.
- **Drug Interactions,** a knowledge base derived from the Medispan system
- **PDQ,** Physicians Data Query, which has approximately 1,000 cancer treatment protocols approved by the National Cancer Institute.
- **Medical Facts File,** a database developed in-house of pertinent medical information, and authoritative sources that users can check when seeking basic knowledge. The first module is instructions-to-authors for journal publications.

Research Databases
- **Molecular Biology Databases:** These are a series of systems comprising the Protein Identification Registry (PIR) and the NIH GenBANK. Our package includes GCG, a special sequencing software system developed at the University of Wisconsin to allow scientists to conduct sequence matching computations.
- **Research-in-Progress:** This module includes the annual Faculty Publications at Georgetown. We are developing a Registry of faculty research and interest profiles.

Diagnostic Systems
- **RECONSIDER:** A diagnostic prompting system based on the AMA, CMIT 8th edition and developed by the University of California, San Francisco
- **DXplain,** an up-to-date diagnostic system developed at Massachusetts General Hospital, Harvard University.
- **QMR and ILIAD** are two other stand-alone systems not yet linked to our network, but used for teaching purposes.

5.3 Macintosh Interface

An icon-based interface to facilitate user access was recently completed. The first phase provides access to miniMEDLINE, which features a pull-down memo, and multiple windows. Similar interfaces to the OPAC and ALERTS/CURRENT CONTENTS are under development. This module will serve as a testbed for a graphics based system in the future (figure 4-5).

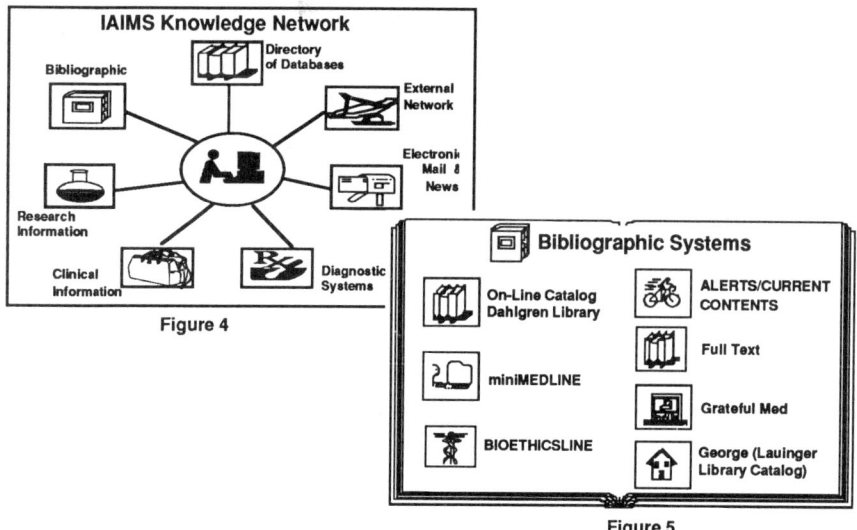

Figure 4

Figure 5

6. LIBRARY SYSTEM FOR THE FUTURE

What began as a system designed to meet the needs of the Dahlgren Library at Georgetown has been shared with other institutions since 1982. Today over 40 libraries use LIS or a portion of it such as miniMEDLINE (Table 1).

• Albert Einstein College of Medicine	• St. John's Medical Center
• Audie Murphy Medical Center	• Southern Illinois University
• Catherine McAuley Health Center	• SUNY - Buffalo
• Cornell University Medical College	• Texas College of Osteopathic Medicine
• Eastern Virginia Medical School	• Texas Tech University
• George Washington University	• Thomas Jefferson University
• Georgetown University	• University of Medicine & Dentistry of NJ
• Hahnemann University	• University of Nebraska Medical Center
• Henry Ford Hospital	• University of South Carolina
• Medical College of Georgia	• University of Tennessee, Memphis
• Medical University South Carolina	• University of Texas, San Antonio
• Memorial Sloan-Kettering Cancer Center	• University of Texas, Tyler
• Montefiore Medical Center	• University of Virginia
• Morehouse School of Medicine	• Upjohn Corporation
• OrthoPharmaceutical Corporation	• Winthrop University Hospital
• Payne Whitney Clinic	• Yale University
• Rush/Presbyterian/St. Luke's Medical Ctr	

Table 1: Health Sciences Libraries Using LIS

LIS continually pioneers and explores new means of achieving the totally electronic library. The flexible, open approach of LIS has enabled us to extend our capabilities beyond anything imagined ten years ago. This is why, we advise librarians to emphasize a visionary approach when selecting a library system. It is important to think beyond library services that are provided today, and think strategically about the role the library will play tomorrow. Decisions libraries make today are a stepping stone to the future. That is why librarians should ally themselves to system developers that have a proven futuristic commitment. If you acquire a system that is trying to "catch-up", you are guaranteeing that your library will not be among the leaders in your community. Also, you run the risk that other divisions in your institution will provide computer services that could rightfully belong to the library.

We know the approach at Georgetown works and others seem to agree. Overall, over 250 national and international health professionals visit the library annually to see LIS and its unique features. Considerable time and effort is devoted to sharing knowledge about Georgetown's experience, and to monitoring and modifying LIS to achieve the highest level of excellence. The system is continuously sought by libraries planning to automate. The activity around the library is extensive, often more than can be handled comfortably, but it is also exciting and personally rewarding.

7. ACKNOWLEDGEMENTS

LIS, the miniMEDLINE SYSTEM and ALERTS are trademarks of Georgetown University. CURRENT CONTENTS is a registered trademark of the Institute of Scientific Information.

The IAIMS project is partially supported by NIH Grant No. 5G08LM044392-02 from the National Library of Medicine.

The author wishes to thank Shoukoufeh Larijani for developing the charts and preparing the entire manuscript.

8. REFERENCES

1. Jones, C. Lee, and Deanna B. Marcum. "Integrated Systems: From Library to Campus and Beyond." Bulletin of the Medical Library Association 7, No.3, P. 338-342, July 1983.

2. "A Biotechnology and Biomedical Knowledge Network: IAIMS at Georgetown University Medical Center." A brochure. Washington, DC, 16 pp. August 1988.

3. Broering, Naomi C. "The miniMEDLINE SYSTEM (TM): A Library-based End-User Search System." Bulletin of the Medical Library Association 73, No. 2, P. 138-145, April 1985.

4. Broering, Naomi C. "The Georgetown University Library Information System (LIS): A Mini-computer-based Integrated Library System." Bulletin of the Medical Library Association 71, No.3, p. 317-323, July 1983.

5. Broering, Naomi C. "An Affordable Microcomputer Library Information System Developed by Georgetown University." Microcomputers for Information Management 1, No. 4, P. 269-283, December 1984.

6. Broering, Naomi C. "Emergence of an Electronic Library: A Case Study of the Georgetown University Library Information System." Science and Technology Libraries 5 No. 4, p. 1-10, 1985.

7. Broering, Naomi C and Cannard, Bonnie. "Building Bridges LIS-IAIMS-BioSYNTHESIS." Special Libraries, 79(4), p. 302-313, Fall 1988.

METHODOLOGY FOR DETERMINING DATABASE INTEGRITY FOR YOUR NEWLY LOADED DATABASE: ERROR DETECTION AND RESOLUTION

Cass Brush, St. Francis College

Keywords: Database Conversion, Data Analysis, Local Integrated Systems, Card Print Profiles, Local Location Codes, Project Design.

Abstract: St. Francis College has been cataloging on OCLC since 1978. A grant for retrospective conversion of the philosophy and religion portions of the collection enabled the institution to add around 20,000 records to the database. The collection of 180,000 volumes (around 140,000 titles) is about 20% converted. Innovative Interfaces INNOPAC/INNOVAC system was selected by the library as an integrated in-house system in 1990. In August of that year, the archival tape from OCLC was loaded to the database. Early in November an additional 398 records were loaded to the database. This paper will explore the methodology used to evaluate the integrity of the database, specific examples of things that can turn up externally as well as internally in the review process and hopefully provide some insights into embarking on the evaluation process. The tools, environments, past procedures, current procedures and the basis for all of these will be enumerated and analyzed.

Initial review of the database was accomplished by matching the shelflist cards to the shelflist sort online in the local system. We'll discuss the parameters of this comparison as well as the conclusions leading to the use of other tools for analysis.

Local input problems generic to project-oriented catalog departments, (are there catalog departments that aren't?) will be covered along with their resolution. Qualitative, quantitative, chronological and hierarchical methods of analysis will be specified as well as the individual problems they illuminated or stemmed from. Resolution methods will address specific problems as well as attempt to provide some heuristics for dealing with the types of problems generated by bibliographic records in the MARC format.

1. INTRODUCTION

The library has been cataloging on OCLC since 1978. An off-site recon project added another 20,000 records to the OCLC database. The Pennsylvania Union List of Serials subset of the OCLC Union List of Serials has full serial holdings information for the periodical and serial collection.

The microenhancer on OCLC was used to transmit edited records to the system in batch during non-peak hours. The reports listing records transmitted, dates and errors were retained and filed after the errors were corrected. The archive tapes from

OCLC and the tape of the PaULS local data records for serials were sent to a tape conversion vendor in Pennsylvania, Library Technologies Incorporated. They converted the tapes according to our automation vendor's specifications, ran authority control and generated smart barcodes for records on the tape not in the Reference or Periodicals collection. Dummy barcodes were inserted into reference records' items to create items. The tapes were then sent to Innovative Interfaces in Berkeley where they were loaded into a local system for the library.

The database represented 12 years of cataloging and recon accomplished and supervised by a variety of people with varying levels of professional background. In that there is no individual record access on OCLC, the load presented the staff with a first time look at the database as a whole. The card catalog was evidence of what the records had looked like at one time. There had been several instances of card entries being "whited out" and changed as the book was reclassified with no subsequent update to OCLC. The book matched the cards and the database was remote; a cataloging tool with no visceral connection to the collection. The need to keep the database updated was not conveyed adequately to all members of the staff due to frequent staff and professional changes during the full implementation period. As a result, many of the smart barcodes had no apparent matching entry on the shelves.

The barcoding project was completed during the summer before the database was loaded. Around 35,000 barcodes were generated and 30K of them were matched to the book. The remaining barcodes were kept with the error report sheets from the project in call number order. Barcode project cleanup began as soon as the project was finished. Call numbers were checked in the shelflist to be sure they were correct. A barcode with no matching entry for call number in the shelflist was taken to the author and/or title catalog to determine the correct call number for the record. As soon as the system was installed, we could wand the barcodes in to determine problems with missing call numbers, inaccurate location codes, etc.

The tools used to analyze the load were the local database, the shelflist, original cataloging worksheets, the microenhancer reports, the OCLC database, the packing slip from the tape created by the data conversion vendor and the smart barcodes.

2. <u>METHODOLOGY FOR INITIAL ANALYSIS -- QUANTITATIVE</u>

2.1 The Shelflist Review

In order to determine the percentage of the records written to the archive tapes on OCLC that were loaded to the database, staff began with the shelflist. Call number browse in INNOPAC facilitated review of the shelflist with a mirror image online. Since the tapes that were loaded were generated in March of 1990, any computer generated cards with a date later than March 15 were discounted as candidates by virtue of not being on the loaded tapes. The cards that were sent out for off-site conversion had the OCLC number written on them as an indication that holdings had been added on OCLC. Thus, every card in the shelflist drawers initially examined, (and eventually every card in the shelflist) had to be looked at to determine: 1) if it were computer produced or not, 2) if computer produced, when, 3) if not, was an OCLC number indicated on the card? The following flow chart was quickly assimilated by the staff.

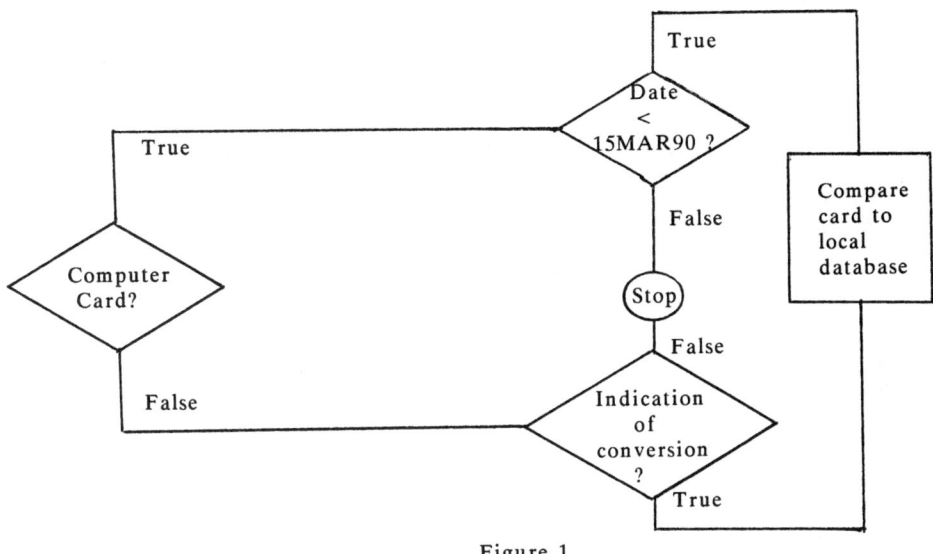

Figure 1

Each card in 60 drawers of the shelflist was reviewed to determine:

a) if it was a candidate for membership in the database
b) if it was present in the database

The comparison was from the shelflist to the database. Holding codes for special collections are stored as locations rather than parts of the call numbers. Therefore, classification numbers assigned to books in the general, reference, rare, etc. collections, all file together. The general collection was used for the base sample. If a candidate with the call number indicated by the shelflist was not present, it was searched in the database by the other indexes: OCLC number, title, etc. to determine if the call number was input incorrectly or altered after card generation. The latter were easy to distinguish because the shelflist card had been altered. In cases where the alternate indexes retrieved no record for the item in the local database, the OCLC number on the conversion cards was noted. For the computer produced cards, the OCLC number and the produce date were noted. The number of records missing from the sample indicated we had a problem.

2.2 <u>Analysis Of The Problem</u>

An analysis of the produce dates on the listing of OCLC numbers indicated a clumping towards the later months, specifically records produced since September of 1989. The first point of error was an output. Had our conversion vendor actually updated holdings for the cards that were annotated? Had we inadvertently deleted holdings for computer produced cards?

OCLC verification

We searched the list of OCLC numbers on OCLC to be sure holdings were attached to the online record for our institution. Printoffs were generated for the records, most of which indicated holdings for the institution. (A few of the conversion project items had been annotated but the OCLC record showed no holdings attached.)

A few of the retrieved items had been originally cataloged. As an aside, original cataloging for the past year was searched on the database and was found to be a subgroup of the missing records. We thought perhaps there was some problem with downloading original workforms from the microenhancer and so double checked OCLC on these. The records were in the union catalog and holdings were attached for all of them.

Broadening the sample

In that records with a later produce date seemed to constitute the majority of the missing records, the microenhancer report sheets were used next. The reports from January to March of 1990, the final three months of input, were reviewed by matching the OCLC numbers to INNOPAC. OCLC numbers not found in the database were highlighted. The later-dated reports again showed a marked increase in the percentage of records that were not loaded. Some records, however, were loaded from each run. The numbers from the March runs were skewed because of an effort in March to catalog as many faculty-authored pieces as possible for inclusion in the database. This involved more than the usual amount of original cataloging. Since original cataloging was already a verified subset of the missing records, the March runs would be expected to have more missing records.

Numerical analysis

Comparing the highlighted microenhancer reports with the lists of OCLC numbers from the shelflist review enabled us to spot what seemed to be a lower limit for the actual number. Numbers beginning with 18, 19 and 20 comprised the entire set of missing numbers. We looked in vain for an OCLC number beginning with 17 in the missing numbers. Review of original cataloging added to the union catalog in March showed the highest OCLC numbers at that time to be in the 20's. Careful review of the numbers beginning with 18 determined that the missing numbers were all equal to or higher than 1835XXXX. The highlighted microenhancer reports for the 3 month period were reviewed and corroborated the numeric finding, no 8 digit OCLC numbers with a number above 1835 in the first 4 places were included in the database.

This was not immediately evident in the OCLC browse online in the local system in that the browse augments decimally rather than numerically. The result of this is that 6 and 7 digit numbers file after 8 digit numbers with a lower 6th and 7th digit. Accordingly, there is no end of file after which all missing numbers would have occurred.

Conclusion

A scroll of the OCLC number index in the database revealed there were no 8 digit numbers following 18345090.

2.3 Pinpointing The Source

Our findings indicated that the conversion vendor had attached holdings to most of the records indicated on the shelflist cards and that we still had holdings attached for the records for which we had produced cards. The next possible point of error was the archival tape from OCLC. Were all of the records with our holdings attached included on the tape to the data conversion vendor? How could we determine if the vendor who had done tape conversion for us had received the records on the tape? Smart barcodes had been generated from the tape. If the books that the missing records represented contained smart barcodes, the records had to have been on the tape.

The printouts from the OCLC searches were taken to the title catalog to determine call numbers for the items. The printouts with the call numbers were then taken to the stacks to determine whether or not smart barcodes had been generated for the books. The books all contained smart barcodes generated from the converted archive tapes.

We contacted customer support for our automation vendor at this point with our findings. We learned that the tape was read in OCLC number order. The information that the problem lay in records at the end of the tape helped us interactively to determine that a false end of tape symbol had been read in during the load.

The library director was kept apprised of the analysis as it proceeded. She compared the packing slip from the tape sent from LTI to III with the number of records on the database at the point of load and found there to be a 398 record discrepancy.

2.4 Resolution Of The Problem

The technical assistant at III was able to retrieve the missing records from the end of the tape. The number of records retrieved matched the number we had determined were missing. He copied them to a cassette tape and sent that tape to us to load to the database.

3. METHODOLOGY FOR SECONDARY ANALYSIS -- QUANTITATIVE

We reviewed the newly loaded records from the OCLC number browse, reviewing every 8 digit number higher than 18345090. Some of the item records attached to the newly loaded bibliographic records contained what seemed at first to be random location codes. The location did not match the location in the bibliograhpic record but while the bibliographic record location was invariably gen for general collection, the item locations varied from video to elem to ibm with no apparent pattern. Further review revealed that the default location was changed when a bibliographic record for a location other than the system default location, gen, was loaded. Using the OCLC number browse, we found that when a record was loaded for a videocassette, for example, the location codes of the items for the next two or three bibliographic records loaded, (i.e. the next two or three numerical OCLC numbers), were set to video while the bibliographic records retained the correct code for the piece.

3.1 Resolution Of The Problem

The processing assistant was set the task of examining the 8 digit OCLC numbers following 18345090 and making sure the location code for the item(s) matched those for the bibliographic record. The OCLC browse from the edit function facilitated the process of retrieving and correcting the item records for this portion of the 398 records loaded.

The integrity of our newly loaded records assured, we moved on to examine problems occurring in sets of records.

3.2 Further Qualitative Analysis--The Holding Codes

We began noticing, with the continued review of the shelflist, that an inordinate amount of titles in the general collection were showing up with an item location of oversize elementary. The titles themselves, titles like "Disordered personalities in literature" and "The moral foundations of professional ethics" were evidence that they were not viable candidates for this collection. A review of these records in the MARC format showed them to contain the holding codes PSFS and PSFX in the 049 field. The library had used the code PSFS to generate a series card for records containing a series formerly not traced by the library that was then to be traced. The code PSFX was used to generate an extra shelflist card. Both of these codes were used as a temporary holding code; a means to produce an extra card. In the case of use of either of them, the code was to have been changed back to the original code representing the general or one of the special collections. As a consequence, neither of these codes were given translation locations in the local system. Our database conversion vendor had alerted us to their existance on the tape. We asked him to print us a list of them because we expected them to present a problem. We also asked that no smart barcodes be generated for the records. The holding code that generated the location OVERSIZE ELEMENTARY, (PSF+), was one of the last codes developed by the library for the card print function. We were able to deduce from this information that PSFX and PSFS were read as PSF+ and generated item locations of OVERSIZE ELEMENTARY. We'd asked no smart barcodes be generated for the Reference collection either. Dummy barcodes were inserted in the item records for Reference. The item records for the PSFS collection also indicated barcodes present in the records. Review of a small sample of the books represented by the records demonstrated that these too, were dummy barcodes. Unfortunately, they would have to be replaced with dumb barcodes in that they were members of the circulating collection.

3.3   Holding Code Problem Resolution

We were able to correct the problem quickly and efficiently with III's "lists" and the boolean operators available. We were able to request a list of all item records attached to bibliographic records with a MARC field value of PSFS or PSFX. We were then able to view the records in the list to determine their bibliographic location. They were all in the general collection. We processed the list in Rapid Updating to set item locations equal to gen for General.

We used the printouts of PSFS and PSFX records to retrieve the books from the stacks to replace the dumb barcodes.

4.   **TOOLS FOR ANALYSIS**

Employing the hindsight that this project has endowed us with, I'd say we learned that the first step in the analysis of the integrity of a database is to recognize possible tools. Assemble all possible sources of data. In this case, the cards were the products of the union catalog as were the holdings statements on that system. The microenhancer reports, while only containing OCLC numbers, proved valuable in the identification of the missing records. The barcodes represented the work done by the tape conversion vendor and were evidence that the records were on the tape. The information that the records were read into the database from the tape in OCLC number order helped us to formulate a theory.

The packing slip of the tape sent from LTI and management information on our local system gave us the actual number of records we were dealing with. All of the above mentioned sources together with careful analysis provided the solution to our problem. Excellent vendor support provided a speedy resolution.

4.1   Manipulating The Tools

Quantitative analysis

The dates and the number ranges had to be intellectually separated from their function as unique record codes in the system and analyzed numerically to yield the solution to the cause of the missing records. The fact that they augmented numerically, were loaded in order numerically and appeared locally in a decimal sort all had to be factored in to see the problem.

Qualitative analysis

Determining the cause for the apparently random location codes generated by the load of the missing records involved seeing an imposed hierarchy in the order of the records. The pattern became apparent only when the records were viewed in relation to one another, i.e. in OCLC number order, in the database.

The problems with the second load, their resolution and the problems with the unspecified holding codes were solved by looking at as many facets of the records as necessary to determine the cause of the problem. The unspecified holding codes were evident to those of us who'd been using the other cataloging codes for card production and realized that they should not have been in the last time use record on the archival tape. A single field within the record was the key to the resolution of this problem.

In both cases, the sophisticated design and ease with which the local system is maintained, enabled us to resolve the problems quickly and easily and return to the inherent problems of a largely unconverted collection.

5. **FUTURE PLANS**

We're continuing the conversion of the collection. We're about 30% converted now and continuing to convert "on the fly" at circulation, process flagged cards from the off-site conversion project, and finish up the cleanup on the barcode project. We're maintaining the shelflist because of the unconverted portion of the collection but the card catalogs are shrinking as cards for deleted books are pulled. New cataloging as well as conversion is being exported directly into the local system from PRISM on OCLC. We feel we were well equipped to deal with the problems that arose. The combination of motivated and problem-oriented staff, an extremely flexible local system and excellent vendor support will enable us to deal with future problems as effectively as we were able to deal with these.

THE UNSEEN POWER BEHIND THE INTEGRATED SYSTEM: A COMPARISON OF VARIOUS OPERATING SYSTEMS

Mary H. Casey, Information Systems Consultants, Inc.

Keywords: Operating Systems, Virtual Storage, Paging, Segmentation, Integrated Online Library Systems, CPU Scheduling.

Abstract: The operating system used by the vendors of integrated online library systems provides the power behind the system. Among the ways the operating system impacts the library functionality is in the manner that instructions and data are brought into the main memory for processing and the scheduling algorithms used to determine the order these processes gain control of the CPU. A comparison of several operating systems is made.

      Although few librarians investigate the operating system of the integrated online library system, it is the operating system that makes possible the many functions of the system. It is truly the power behind the system.
      The operating system is analogous to the conductor of the symphony orchestra. He has before him the printed music with instructions as to tempo and force. The operating system's music is the applications software that instructs the operating system what to do and how to do it. So the conductor calls in the violins and the horns to perform the music, the operating system instructs the CPU to search the database.
      The operating system is an interface between the applications software [i.e., the software written by the vendor] and the hardware. The hardware consists of the Central Processing Unit (CPU), primary and secondary memory, input and output (I/O) media and the connection channels among these items.
      Software is the set of instructions that tells the computer to do what the computer is designed to do. These instructions are usually written in a high level language (one of the functions of the operating system is to provide compilers to translate the high level instructions into machine language). The operating system itself is software, most of which is written in high level language that necessitates an optimizing compiler; however, some operating systems may also have components of firmware. Firmware is instructions to the hardware in microcode--a language below machine language. Firmware instructions are stored in ROM.

1. ORGANIZATION OF THE OPERATING SYSTEM

   Most operating systems are arranged in a hierarchical structure with the kernel or core as the base of the system. The core section resides in main memory or ROM. Other operating system programs are stored in secondary storage media and called into main memory when they are needed to instruct the CPU. The kernel divides main memory into memory partitions, creates processes, synchronizes processes, handles communications between processes and supports the I/O activities, file structures and the accounting functions.
   The operating system functions that are not part of the kernel include the I/O controller, the scheduling controller, the disk storage controller, the file system, security and many utility functions such as backup, copying and moving files. Utilities also supply editing functions and keep track of the use from various terminals, frequency of mistakes and various other reporting functions.
   The operating system is a complicated subject that could consume days or pages of analysis. However, there are two areas that warrant discussion and comparison when the power of the operating system is the subject. These are the ability of the operating system to make the hardware virtual storage and the manner in which the scheduling of work is accomplished within the computer system.
   The library automation products are judged by librarians and patrons in a variety of different ways. Chief among them is response time which is directly impacted by the algorithms used to bring data and instructions into main memory and schedule the processing of the data and instructions.

2. VIRTUAL STORAGE

   All of the operating systems that this paper addresses provide virtual storage or virtual memory. Virtual storage implies that the user sees space on secondary storage media as main memory. This allows the system to run programs that are too large to fit into primary storage; programs must be in primary storage or in cache storage in order for the CPU to access them for processing.
   The operating system divides the program processes into blocks called pages or segments that can be swapped in and out of main memory. The operating system assigns all blocks a virtual address. When the blocks are swapped into main memory the virtual addresses are mapped into the real addresses of main memory.
   Bringing the blocks into main memory requires that there be a placement strategy for their location in main memory. "Best-fit" implies that the incoming block is placed in the main memory hole that is closest to its size; "first-fit" dictates that the block go to the first available partition that is large enough to support it.

2.1 Paging

   The operating system accomplishes this mapping of virtual addresses to real addresses through a function called dynamic address translation (DAT). This function also maintains an address translation map that indicates the real addresses of all the virtual addresses that are located in main memory. Of course, the addresses are those of a block. Blocks of the same size are called pages and are usually 512 bytes. Segments are used by some systems. Segments are hardware defined partitions in main memory and are multiples of the page size defined through memory address partitioning.

The page map is an important item in library automation. It is this function that enables many users to execute the same programs and share data. Pure procedures (those that cannot be modified) can have pointers in the page map to nonmodifiable data. Many pure procedures may have pointers to the same data. In the case of modifiable data, the operating system provides a mutual exclusion algorithm which provides that only one procedure may access data to modify it at one time.

Unlike pages, segments are entire processes or even a program which contain not only code and data but some information about the segment including access rights and storage protection information.

Placement of pages or segments in main memory has no particular spatial requirements. Contiguous blocks in virtual storage need not be contiguous in real storage. Placement of pages is easy since all partitions are the same size, a page will occupy any vacant partition. Segments enter main memory using the best-fit or first-fit strategies.

2.2   Page Displacement Algorithms

Page replacement or displacement is a more complicated issue. A decision must be made as to which page to displace to make room for a new page. The object is to displace a page that will not be needed again.

There are several popular page displacement strategies: (1) First In First Out (FIFO) replaces the page that arrived first in main memory; however, it may also be the most used; (2) Least Frequently Used displaces the page that has been used the least; however, this may be the last page to arrive in main memory and not necessarily the one that will not be used again; (3) Not Used Recently (NUR) displaces the page that has not been used recently. This is accomplished through the use of reference and modification bits attached to the pages. The bits identify references (0 indicates the page has not been referenced, 1 identifies a referenced page) and modifications (0 indicates no modifications, 1 identifies a page that has been modified).

Displacing a page that has been modified requires that the page be written to secondary storage, this is not required of a nonmodified page. So it is obvious that replacing a nonmodified page is preferable. In fact, the hierarchy for displacement using this NUR strategy is unreferenced and unmodified, unreferenced and modified, referenced and unmodified and, if no other choice, referenced and modified. Periodically, all reference bits are reset to zero.

Some operating systems bring into main memory or cache only the pages that are demanded. Others bring in pages that are nearby following the theory that if a page is needed that those nearby are also likely to be needed.

The impact that paging has on the response time of an integrated online library system cannot be overemphasized. Bringing pages into main memory takes time. In most hardware platforms the CPU time used to accomplish this function is nil because most systems have a direct memory access chip. This chip enables the computer to transfer information between secondary and main memory without the CPU having to take over this function; the CPU is free to continue processing.

2.3   Various Operating Systems Paging Techniques

As was noted before most operating systems use a 512 byte page and assign virtual addresses to all programs and data stored in all storage media. The exception to this rule is IBM's MVS. MVS is an operating system for the IBM mainframes, it can sit alone on a computer or be hosted by the VM operating system.

MVS uses a system of segments composed of 64K and each segment is further divided into pages of 4K (4,096) bytes. Only pages that are needed are swapped into main memory. This process is called demand paging. Pages are kept in main memory only when they are active. The system also provides a buffer for the most recently used pages to be held making them available for reuse.

The PICK operating system uses the 512 byte pages and pages into main memory on demand. Pages are displaced on the basis of the least used method. PICK is gradually becoming used primarily as a part of the operating system database management system and has always been popular because of its database capabilities. At this point most vendors who use PICK are mounting it on top of UNIX which has the same size pages but uses a NUR or Not Used Recently algorithm for page displacement--a more efficient method than the simple least used method.

Digital's VAX/VMS divides its storage areas into 512 byte pages and swaps into main memory all pages needed for a particular program at the beginning of the processing of the program.

Hewlett-Packard's MPE uses paged virtual memory. It fetches pages from secondary storage in groups using the principle of locality. Locality dictates that when one page is needed, others contiguous to it will also be needed so they are also brought into main memory. Frequently used pages are stored in main memory for future use.

3.   SCHEDULING

The CPU is capable of processing the many requests which are necessitated by the use of multiple terminals in an integrated online environment. However, in order to do this a complicated method of scheduling must be employed.

All the operating systems covered in this discussion are multiprogramming; that is, they have in main memory multiple instructions and data to be processes and the control of the CPU goes from one to the other so that it appears to the user as simultaneous processing. Within the broad classification of multiprogramming are several related terms: multitasking implies that a single program will have within it several separate but interrelated tasks; multi-user implies that there are multiple ports on the system and they are serviced concurrently; and, timesharing implies a method used to allow several users to access the same program concurrently.

3.1 Scheduling Algorithms

In the multiprogramming environment, processes in main memory gain control of the CPU in order to run by a specific algorithm that is part of the scheduling controller of the operating system. Some of these algorithms are: First In First Out (FIFO), Shortest Job First (SJF), Round Robin, Fair Share Scheduling, and the use of multi-level queues. All of these methods fall into two categories: preemptive and nonpreemptive. Preemptive scheduling algorithms allow the operating system to organize use of the CPU. The operating system may set a quantum or otherwise control the length of time that a process retains control of the CPU. In nonpreemptive scheduling the process continues to maintain CPU control until it relinquishes it.

FIFO, a nonpreemptive algorithm, means just what the name implies--the first process that enters main memory or cache is processed first. It maintains control until it issues an interrupt when it needs more data or instructions or the process is completed. Since the first job may be long, the response time for a series of processes may be negatively impacted by this algorithm.

SJF, a nonpreemptive algorithm, assures the least response time for the shortest job because it is activated first. However, the response time for the longer jobs tends to be unacceptable with this method. Also, in an interactive setting this is impractical because the operating system cannot determine which is actually the shortest job. This method is useful in batch processing or in combination with other methods.

Round Robin uses a ready queue and is preemptive. The first process in the queue is given control of the CPU for a quantum. usually 10 to 100 milliseconds. If the process is not complete in that time it relinquishes control and is moved to the back of the queue. Control is passed to the next process. If a process finishes before the quantum runs out, it issues an interrupt to the operating system which passes control to the next process in the queue.

The multi-level queue is usually a combination of several algorithms. Processes are assigned a foreground or a background queue, depending on priority. Interactive processes are normally assigned the foreground, batch processes, the background. The foreground may be scheduled in the Round Robin method while the background uses the FIFO or SJF mode. No process in the background queue runs until the foreground queue is empty. Some operating systems allow for movement of processes from one queue to another, others do not. Some operating systems which use the Round Robin algorithm in the foreground queue increase the duration of the quantum assigned to a long process each time it gains control of the CPU.

Fair Share Scheduling employs a Round Robin algorithm but also develops several queues with differing priorities.

3.2 Various Operating Systems Scheduling Algorithms

UNIX uses the Fair Share Scheduling algorithm employing multiple queues and using the Round Robin algorithm to select the process to run.

Digital's VMS uses a system of multiple queues as does UNIX but usually many more priority queues are employed. Processes are assigned a quantum but the running process may issue an interrupt when it has need for input or output (I/O).

IBM's MVS uses a hierarchy for selection of the task to activate through the use of address selection. Once a particular address is chosen for control of the CPU the highest priority task residing at that address in the ready queue is given control of the CPU.

Hewlett-Packard's MPE uses a priority queue that divides tasks into five priority classes (four foreground and one background). Once a process gains control of the CPU it maintains it until it issues an interrupt. The control then passes to the next highest priority process; if two processes have the same priority, the oldest process is activated.

4. CONCLUSION

Although there is no "right" operating system just as there is no "right" integrated online library system, the operating system should be investigated by the librarian who is making a selection of an online vendor. As shown, this element has the ability to add significantly to the functionality of the automated system.

INTEGRATING EXTERNAL FILES INTO AN ONLINE CATALOG: COMPARATIVE SEARCH STRATEGIES

Kellian D. Clink, Mankato State University

ABSTRACT: At Mankato State University, the online catalog has become a vehicle for searching ERIC. This is the first of several external files that will be added to MSUS/PALS, including Books for College Libraries III, Psychological Abstracts, and LC Authority files. Others in the negotiation stages are some Wilson indexes, currently available as a test file, and a government publication file. ERIC's current availability has been seen as a trial run, and MSUS/PALS has actively solicited reference staff response to this new development. At Mankato State University's Memorial Library, ERIC has been available to patrons through paid mediated searches, available on Dialog OnDisc at no charge to the patron, and now is available on all online catalogs at no cost to the patron. The author uses her own experience using ERIC on MSUS/PALS as well as teaching ERIC on MSUS/PALS to students in the classroom and on the reference desk to assess advantages and pitfalls of having this standard source available on the online catalog as it is currently configured.

1. Introduction

In the fall of 1990, MSUS/PALS added an external file, the Educational Resources Information Center, ERIC, to the online catalogs of all of the 48 libraries connected by MSUS/PALS. ERIC is used primarily by educators but has fairly broad coverage and serves many students who are doing papers for composition and mass communication classes. Mankato State University serves over 15,000 students, those taking education classes accounting for about ten percent of total credits generated in 1989-90. A third of the credits generated by the College of Education are in graduate credit hours.[1] Thus, there is a compelling need to serve graduate education students with ERIC. In the past, ERIC searches for graduate students constituted a major part of our fee-based database searching. The graduate students that we serve, in my experience, are teachers coming back to do graduate work. They are frequently pressed for time, intimidated by the technological aspects of libraries, but eager to learn and explore their subjects.

ERIC is a database divided into an indexing service of over 750 journals (Current Index to Journals in Education--CIJE) and an index to research reports of interest to educators (Resources in Education--RIE). The RIE part of ERIC tends to be papers presented at conferences, doctoral dissertations, practicum papers, speeches, position papers, evaluation instruments, masters theses, etc). Memorial Library purchased ERIC on Dialog OnDisc in the fall of 1989, after trials had determined that users found this very user-friendly and helpful in their research. At the same time, we discontinued InfoTrac and added 5 other compact discs, including Marcive, Compact Disclosure, UMI's Newspaper Abstracts OnDisc, Periodical Abstracts OnDisc, and PsycLit on Silver Platter. When Memorial Library added both ERIC and PsycLit on compact disc, the demand for mediated database searching dropped off dramatically and reference questions increased exponentially. It was felt, however, that having students able to conduct their searches independently was advantageous to their learning experience and worth the extra time at the compact disc stations. Students, with able assistance, can explore more related topics and combine subjects in new and interesting ways on compact disc. Graduate students using our mediated search services had been limited by their budgets, in most cases, from exploring topics the way they can on compact disc. Having the database available on compact disc did pose a problem, though, in that students had to schedule themselves for 20-30 minute time slots due to high demand and it was sometimes difficult for them to find an available slot. In the fall of 1990, ERIC became available on all the online catalog terminals in the library, and ERIC via Dialog OnDisc was discontinued, which meant access for a larger number of students at any one time.

The literature reveals other schools' experiences with adding external files on their online catalogs. Many schools, including Loyola University and Arizona State University, added many of the Wilson databases because of the large number of students who use them. Many medical libraries have added Medline. MSUS/PALS chose to start with ERIC because of its high use and low price. Many librarians at Mankato State University felt that students can use the Wilson indexes in print format very effectively for their level of information seeking behavior. Databases made available in compact disc, and now on MSUS/PALS, were those that were highly used in our mediated-search services. Fee-based database searches were done primarily for upper-division and graduate students with sophisticated information needs. These needs were met by the power of boolean operators, the ability to search for terms adjacent to one another, and the ability to modify sets.

David Cohen has pointed to the desirability of integrating searches for both articles and books in his article, "Scholarly Communication and the Role of Libraries." He points to a study done by the American Council of Learned Societies that found scholars "do not rate libraries high on the list of resources required for their research and they are not using the new technologies that libraries offer for accessing information."[2] He has several suggestions for improving access including many improvements that ERIC on MSUS/PALS offers. He proposes an online catalog which allows the patron to find books, articles, films, etc in the same format with the same "search engine" which would have keyword access with boolean operators.[3] While some of these improvements are attained by the use of CD-ROMS, he notes the difficulties patrons experience with searching CD-ROMS--their confusion with the subject focus, and the lack of standard search methodologies and displays. He would like MSUS/PALS. It has allowed students to find articles, books, videos, films, journal titles, and government documents, all using the same user-friendly, very flexible search commands.

2. Public Relations

The College of Education's faculty members were informed that ERIC had become available as an external file in the fall, to facilitate assignment-making. ERIC on Dialog OnDisc had been used extensively for assignments and we wanted to allow faculty members to change their assignments to ask the students to use ERIC via MSUS/PALS instead of the compact disc. In addition, drop-in sessions were held to help faculty learn to use ERIC on MSUS/PALS. In handouts and at the desk, the metaphor of a file cabinet is used: our students are told that they must close one drawer (the online catalog) before being able to open another (ERIC). It is a difficult concept for our patrons to grasp, partially because the concept of book, journal, and journal article are not sometimes not well-defined in the students' minds. A brochure was created that includes search tips, descriptions of commands to search specific fields, the mandatory "Educational Level Descriptors," and printing instructions.

Students must type **FILE ERIC** or **FILE JIE** or **FILE RIE** to access either the full ERIC database, the Current Index to Journal Articles or Research in Education, respectively. Typing **FILE CAT** or **BE** returns the user to the online catalog. Currently, students must return to the online catalog to establish journal issue availability, although linking the online catalog and ERIC is somewhere in the future. Once in one of the ERIC files, the online catalog's commands are used to look for sources.

3. Searching ERIC on MSUS/PALS

MSUS/PALS is very powerful, flexible, and easy for students to use, for the most part. Students can search ERIC using term search (**TE**), subject searching (**SU**), subject term searching (**ST**), and author searching (**AU**). Truncation is achieved by using the pound (**#**) sign. Once patrons find some desired resources, they can restrict their search by adding other concepts or by limiting by year (they can also limit by year on the same line), or by limiting by a title term which will search the article and journal title. It is possible to use boolean operators both between individual words or between set numbers created by saving (**SA**) a search. MSUS/PALS does these operations in the order entered. Therefore, if one does a search for example, **TE migrants or migrant or migratory and urban**, MSUS/PALS works to find sources on (migrants or migrant or migratory) and urban. Students can also create sets and then combine them, for example **TE migrants or migrant or migratory**, **SA** (to save that set, which would be assigned set number 1), and then do a term search for any synonym for urban, so they would type **TE urban or cities or suburban , SA** (to save that set, which would be assigned set number 2) and then do separate sets for individual cities, such as **TE Minneapolis or Duluth or Moorhead**, **SA** (creating set 3) and then combine sets: **BO 2 or 3 and 1**. Again, MSUS/PALS performs the boolean operators in the order received, so this set would contain the sources with the names of the cities or the words city or urban or suburban that also had the words migrants or migrant or migratory. Patrons can prelimit their search by choosing to search the **FILE RIE** or **FILE JIE.**

MSUS/PALS does have some limitations, however. A searcher cannot find two words adjacent to one another, which poses problems when a student needs items on a subject that has not become a descriptor or identifier. Another limitation is that the system maxes out in these two ways--by an approximate 90 second limit and a 9800 records limit. In either case, the system looks alphabetically by title and gives the user the records from the first part of the alphabet. For example, a student looking up education and teaching in ERIC would find that the system responds by saying that education maxed out the system, would find 19,600 records with the words teaching and would come up with 9800 records total. More seriously, perhaps, is the inability to search abstracts. Another limitation is the number and size of sets that can be created. Most of these limitations can be overcome with ingenuity on the part of the searcher--they can do separate searches in the two halves of ERIC--JIE and RIE; they can learn to formulate a very specific search strategy before even getting onto the database, or separate the research question into smaller components; and they can explore the <u>Thesaurus of ERIC Descriptors</u> thoroughly to help them with exactly the right descriptive words. All of this, however, takes time, motivation and perseverance to learn.

I would like to explore in the remainder of this paper the differences between searching ERIC on MSUS/PALS, BRS and Dialog and their compact disc equivalents in an effort to understand the following question: Do students searching ERIC on MSUS/PALS get the kind of comprehensive search they need for a Master's thesis? I am interested in the issue of service to graduate students because, in deciding on CD's and then external files, many of our librarians have felt that printed indexes often meet the needs of undergraduates and it is our upper-level and graduate students whose needs are best met with new technology. My student for the following example is starting to look for information about media and migrants. This hypothetical student is just starting out and is more interested in recall than precision. This student might start by trying the following strategy:
FILE ERIC
TE migrant or migrants
SA (to save the set--it is assigned set number 1)
TE radio or media or television or video
SA (saves the set as set number 2)

However, the student notices that the system maxes out in the second set after media. It finds 2809 for radio, then when it **or**s the media, comes to its own maximum number of hits--9800 and while it states that it **or**'s television or video, it has already reached its maximum capacity before this point. The student realizes that s/he is really only getting migrant or migrants and radio and part of the articles that have the word media in them. If the student has used the system frequently, s/he might think to go back and do the following steps:

TE migrant or migrants
SA (to be able to reuse this set number 1 for combination with the other concepts)
and radio (creates a set of (migrant or migrants) and radio)
SA (saves the set and assigns it set number 2)
GE 1 (to get migrant or migrants back)
and media
SA (creates set number 3)
GE 1
and television
SA (creates set number 4)
GE 1
and video
SA (creates set number 5)
BO 2 or 3 or 4 or 5
GT 1982 (to limit the search to articles/documents written after 1982)
DI

WHEW! The student could look then look at the resulting list of 11 items.

On BRS, the searcher would need to do the following:
(migrant or migrants) and (radio or media or television or video)
..l/1 yr > 82

On ERIC on Silver Platter, the student would press the F2 key. They would type after the FIND: **(migrant or migrants) and (radio or media or television or video)** and the combine that set number with **PY=1983:1990**

On Dialog, the searcher would need to enter this strategy:
SS (migrant or migrants) and (radio or media or television or video)
ss s10 and py=1983:1990

On ERIC on Dialog OnDisc, the searcher would need to use several steps via the menu to 1/Begin the Search, 2/Find and choose the migrant/s,3/Modify the search by alphabetically scanning the index for the radio/media/television/video and choosing them, 4/Displaying the search, and 5/printing the search. This would take, in my opinion, a fairly skilled and determined user. In my experience with users on Dialog OnDisc, users neglected to read and/or understand the menus and frequently didn't understand that the enter key had to be pressed after selecting an option from the menu. Some of our reference librarians were turning to training the students to use the Dialog Command Mode of the product, in which case the student needed to know some command language but could use the same strategy as above.

With the BRS or Dialog or their compact disc equivilents, the student would find more citations than on ERIC on MSU/PALS, because MSUS/PALS does not search abstracts. To study relevancy, I looked at the 11 items found on MSUS/PALS vs. the 38 found on BRS and Dialog. The 11 titles from PALS are the following:

Case Study on Television as a Meeting Place (Federal Republic of Germany).
Construction/Communication and Media
Construccion/Communicacion y Medios Publicitarios
Directory of Australian Multicultural Films and Videos
Language Learning with Laser
Media, Migrants and Marginalization: The Situation in the Federal Republic of Germany

"Migrants and the Media"--from 'Guest Workers' to Linguistic and Cultural Minorities
Preferences of Mexican-American Children for Parents or Television
Public Policy and the Migrant Child
The Role of Information in the Realization of the Human Rights of Migrant Workers
The Prevention and Treatment of Child Abuse and Neglect: A Focus on the Mexican-American
    Family

The titles from BRS & DIALOG (not including those already found in PALS):

1988 Washington State Program for Migrant Children's Education
1987 Washington State Program for Migrant Children's Education
1986 Washington State Program for Migrant Children's Education
It's Our Move Now: A Community Action Guide to the UN Nairobi Forward-Looking Stategies for
    the Advancement of Women
National Paired Reading Conference Proceedings
After the Harvest: The Plight of Older Farmworkers
Library Users Whose Second Language is English: A Bibliography of Sources
"Musiques sans frontieres (1987-1988)": An Intercultural Competition
Prejudice and the Reduction of Prejudice in Australian Society
Educational Trends in South Carolina
Biennial Report on Regional Education Service Centers
State Plan for Regional Education Service Centers
Salud/Servicios Personales. Libro de Profesor
Occupational Resources: Career Information (Grade 5)
Occupational Resources: Career Information (Grade 3)
Information Needs of Arabic-Speaking Migrants
Language, Migrants and Power
Chicanos: A Checklist of Current Materials
Hometown Newspaper Coverage of Developing Countries: Its Effects on Perceived
    Interdependence of Nations
Program for Migrant Children's Education
A Resource Guide and Annotated Bibliography on Labor Studies for Students and Teachers in the
    State of Washington
Reaching Out: The Role of Audio Cassette Communication in Rural Development
Health/Personal Services B2. CHOICE: Challenging Options in Career Education
Project of National Significance for Providing Advocacy Services to Hispanic and Asian
    Developmentally Disabled Persons Residing in California
Hispanic Behavioral Science Research: Recommendations for Future Research
Migrant Child Education. Learning Activities Direct Instruction K-8
Oregon State University College Assistance Migrant Program Performance Report
Case Study on Hajitkoum, Migrant Cultural Action Group
Economies Gained by Sharing Resources

Some of these citations would probably not be of interest to my hypothetical student. As always with searching, sometimes both words are in the record, but the connection between them doesn't exist as the student would like. Some of the citations above are to career kits for migrant children, including some about becoming media professionals. The searcher might eliminate these. However, of the 28 citations not found via MSUS/PALS, 16 seem like articles that the student definitely would want to review, judging their content on the information provided in the abstract. They include the state-specific citations about migrant education, the article on library users, the report entitled "Language, Migrants, and Power," the checklist of current materials in Chicano Area Studies, the document entitled "Program for Migrant Children's Education," the paper on "Reaching Out," the conference report "The Role of Information in the Realization of the Human Rights of Migrant Workers," one on learning activities, and the "Case Study on Hajitkoum Migrant Cultural Action Group."

The reason that these citations were not retrieved with MSUS/PALS is that the media concept showed up only in the abstract and not in the title of the article or journal or descriptors or identifiers. Other searches that I performed on public radio, on migrants and reading, on migrants and mathematics showed the same deficiency. The inability to search abstracts results in a less than comprehensive search which does the graduate student a disservice, particularly since it's entirely possible the student won't realize that the search that they've performed is not comprehensive.

Another problem is the inability to use adjacency operators. This lack can cause students to retrieve irrelevant hits, as they can only AND words. One example is the patron looking for articles about public radio. There is an identifier (not in the <u>Thesaurus</u>) but not a descriptor (in the <u>Thesaurus</u>) "National Public Radio." The patron might look in the <u>Thesaurus,</u> find nothing on public radio and conclude that they must use term (TE) searching. If the patron knows enough to browse subject headings (**BR SU Public Radio** or **BR SU National Public Radio**), they can find 29 or 24 cites and select (**SE**) them. However, most students don't know about or use the browse commands. If the patron does a term search for public radio (**TE PUBLIC RADIO**) and limits to greater than 1988, (**GT 1988**) they get eight documents, two of which are relevant citations. In BRS or Dialog, the searcher can find these two words next to each other (BRS by typing **public adj radio** and Dialog by typing **public()radio**) and come up with the two relevant citations. In ERIC on MSUS/PALS, the irrelevant hits occur because, to give some examples, an article is retrieved which is about public speaking experience gained by having students do radio shows, one article is about public policy for commerical radio, another is about public opinion about Radio Marti, etc. In BRS, the searcher can create a better tailored bibliography, thus saving the patron money, time, and effort. On Silver Platter and using Dialog Command Mode on Dialog OnDisc, the student (with training) can find words next to one another. Although the subject headings for ERIC are well-developed and can be used to great advantage for many searches, adjacency operators are frequently necessary to obtain the best results. Teaching students when and how to use adjacency operators is, of course, as difficult as it is necessary.

4. Conclusion

In conclusion, I would like to enumerate the many ways that MSUS/PALS is an online catalog with search capabilities appropriate for doing database searching. The features that make it appropriate are: boolean operators, term search capability, internal and end-truncation, and browse capabilities. The concept of using the online as a vehicle for searching indexes to books and different kinds of articles is great. Students can do "one-stop shopping," looking for both articles and books at the same terminal using the same command language, which makes instruction both easier and more important (since they can use the knowledge gained through Bibliographic Instruction sessions for multiple purposes). MSUS/PALS is powerful, flexible, and relatively easy to use.

The current inability to search abstracts, however, makes searching ERIC on MSUS/PALS inadequate, in my opinion, for the purposes of the graduate student seeking a comprehensive literature review on her/his topic. In conversations with Mike Barnett, a programmer for MSUS/PALS, I discovered that it is possible for MSUS/PALS to make available abstract searchability. However, the student would then have even more problems with the system "maxing out"--either by time or by number of hits. The answer may be to prelimit the search, which is technologically feasible. I would propose the creation of a third database, perhaps five years "deep" with all fields searchable. RIE and JIE could continue in their present format, but a current database could be created and called CIE--Currents in Education--and would be completely searchable by descriptors, identifiers, and abstracts. Every year, one year's worth of indexing could be dropped from the fully searchable database and one year added. Adjacency operators could be added without programming difficulty. It appears that the "max out" problems cannot be eliminated except maybe by the creation of this smaller file, which I feel would answer the needs of graduate students, who are most frequently looking for comprehensive results within a five-year span.

This paper has proposed for me as many questions as it answered. I do not feel that we as librarians have a firm grasp on how students are using all of the wonderful products that we are making available to them at great cost. While students at Mankato State Unversity have responded with great enthusiasm to compact discs, and now to ERIC on MSUS/PALS, I cannot feel that they get the kinds of results an experienced database searcher does, as s/he thinks of synonyms and manipulates sets. Some students, at least, get overwhelmed at the very outset and give up. Many professors do not understand how complex information-seeking has become and do not allow adequate time in their courses for bibliographic instruction sessions. I'm still waiting for artificial intelligence to close the gap between the infinite possibilities of the technology and the finite patience of the patrons.

ENDNOTES

1. Institutional Research, Department Credit Hour Summary 1989-1990. Mankato: Mankato State University, 1990.
2. David J. Cohen, "Scholarly Communication and the Role of Libraries: Problems and Possibilities for Accessing Journal Articles," The Serials Librarian 17(3-4): 43-48, 1990.
3. ibid.

BIBLIOGRAPHY

Cochrane, Pauline A. Redesign of Catalogs and Indexes for Improved Online Subject Access: Selected Papers of Pauline A. Cochrane Phoenix, AZ: Oryx Press,1985.

Cohen, David J. "Scholarly Communication and the Role of Libraries: Problems and Possibilities for Accessing Journal Articles." The Serials Librarian 17 (3-4):43-48.

Hendley, Margaret. " Staff Training in an Automated Environment: Keeping the Patron in Mind," Canadian Library Journal 46(2):101-103.

Klemperer, Katharina. "New Dimensions for the Online Cataline: The Dartmouth College Library Experience." Information Technology and Libraries 8 (2):138-145.

Machovec, George S. "Locally Loaded Databases in Arizona State University's Online Catalog Using the CARL System." Information Technology and Libraries 8(2): 161-171.

Rouse, William B., and Sandra H. Rouse and David R. Morehead. "Human Information Seeking: Online Searching of Bibliographic Citation Networks," Information Processing and Management 18(3):141-149.

White, Howard D. and Belver Griffith. "Quality of Indexing in Online Data Bases," Information Processing and Management 23(3):211-224.

THE PUBLIC SERVICES LIBRARIAN AS SYSTEM ADMINISTRATOR

Gregory A. Crawford, Rutgers, The State University of New Jersey

Keywords: System Administrator, Public Services Librarian, Online Library Systems

Abstract: In many small- to medium-sized libraries, library budgets will not support a full-time system administrator for the library's online catalog. In addition, the demands of the system do not justify the expense. Thus, a staff member will usually accept the responsibility of being system administrator in addition to his or her regular duties. This paper examines the advantages and disadvantages of using a Public Services Librarian as the system administrator. The duties of the system administrator include, among others: system maintenance, staff training, troubleshooting, aiding users, and implementing library policies and procedures. Due to their duties within the library, Public Services Librarians are logical choices to fulfill these tasks. They already possess the skills to work with and to educate the library's clientele; they must be cognizant of library policies and procedures; and most are adept at using computers as part of their work. As a result, the Public Services Librarian can be a very effective system administrator.

The system administrator in charge of a library's integrated online system must fulfill many roles. He or she is responsible for the smooth operation of the system and for the translation and implementation of library policies and procedures into automated form. Additionally, the system administrator must work cooperatively and effectively not only with the technical services staff, but also with the public services department and the administration of both the library and the institution. Thus, the system administrator spans departments and often possesses a large amount of de facto power.

Within the small to medium-sized library, both academic and public, library budgets often do not have the funds available for a full-time system administrator. Also, the workload for the system administrator may not justify such an expense. Thus, a current staff member must often perform the tasks of the system administrator in addition to his or her regular duties. This can put a strain on that individual, and often on an entire department, especially during the early stages of automation such as profiling or installation and later during times when problems arise. I believe, however, that for the smaller academic library, using a current staff member as the first system administrator may be far preferable than hiring someone to come into the position from outside the institution.

This paper will discuss the use of a Public Services Librarian as system administrator in the smaller academic library, although most of what will be said applies equally to larger academic libraries and to public libraries. The author's experiences in such a position at Moravian College provide the basis for the discussion of the general responsibilities of the system administrator. In addition, the advantages and disadvantages of using a Public Services Librarian as system administrator will be presented.

Moravian College is a selective liberal arts college with a primarily residential student body of 1200, a graduate theological seminary, and a continuing studies program. The library was committed to automation long before funds became available to make automation a reality. In June, 1986, an anonymous gift of $200,000 was presented to the library for the expressed purpose of pursuing automation. This was followed by a $10,000 grant from the state of Pennsylvania in August, 1986, and an additional $50,000 anonymous gift in June, 1987. As a result of these gifts, the library was able to concentrate on the careful selection of a system which fully met the needs of its users and staff. Proposal evaluations and contract negotiations were completed in the fall of 1988. The system hardware was installed in December 1988; reclassification from Dewey Decimal into Library of Congress Classification, relabelling, barcoding, and shifting of the collection was begun in June, 1989; and the system, except for serials and acquisitions, was operational on September 5, 1989, for the opening of the fall semester. As the director of the automation project, it was natural that I become administrator for the system once it was installed.

The selection of the first system administrator will be an extremely important decision in many ways for the library pursuing automation. This individual will leave his or her fingerprints not only on the system itself, but also upon the operation of the library for years to come. Thus, it is imperative the the selection of the system administrator be considered carefully. A knowledge of library automation in general is useful, although a willingness to learn may be of greater benefit. Most important, however, is a knowledge of both the library itself, including its procedures, policies, goals, and limitations, and the users of the library, including the students, staff, and faculty. As a result, the selection of a current staff member as the first system administrator has many advantages.

If a current staff member can be chosen for the position of system administrator, that individual should be involved as much as possible in the planning for the system, its selection, and its implementation. This will provide the primary advantage of participating in the entire development of the project and will give a more comprehensive understanding of not only the hardware but also the rationale behind many of the decisions that must be made.

Planning for automation can be very time-consuming, yet, if this stage is approached carefully, a much better system will result. Planning should include a thorough analysis of library needs and how it is envisioned that automation will assist daily operations and improve library service to patrons. For example, what services are provided that are little used or that cause frustration on the part of users? Which services are valued greatly by patrons? By asking such questions, a better understanding of how automation will affect the library can be achieved. Decisions made at the planning stage will have great influence on the rest of the automation project. It is at the planning stage that many decisions, such as the following, will be made: the number of terminals needed and their placement, the modules of the software to be purchased and the order in which will they be implemented, changes in policies and procedures, effects on staff, etc. Each of these decisions influences the ultimate configuration and operation of the library's computerized system. By involving the future system administrator in the planning for the system, his or her understanding of the goals of the whole project will be increased greatly.

The selection of a library system brings with it a chance to learn a great deal about the library automation marketplace and library automation in general. During this phase of the project, vendor literature must be read carefully to learn the capabilities and limitations of various systems. In addition, visits to libraries which have installed the systems being considered for purchase can prove very enlightening. These informal meetings often yield much useful information such as working relationships with vendors, software or hardware deficiencies, hints on profiling, training methods, etc. At this time, the system administrator will be able to learn how other libraries have set up their systems, how their operations have been affected, and other benefits and limitations of automation.

Involvement in the implementation of the library system increases the system administrator's technical competence by exposing him or her to the installation of both the hardware and the software. By working with the vendor during this process, knowledge of the system and of the company itself is gained. Personal contacts with vendor employees may be very beneficial later when difficulties arise. Implementation inevitably brings with it problems, both in the hardware and in the software. Trouble-shooting of these problems increases the system administrator's knowledge of the machinery and the programs.

By being actively involved in all phases of the planning, selection, and implementation of the system, the system administrator will possess a larger view of the system and its place within the functioning of the library. The system is not seen just as a conglomeration of hardware which must be monitored, but as an integral part of the day to day services provided by the library to its staff and patrons.

The most important stage of system implementation in which the system administrator should be involved is that of the profiling of the software and the configuration of the hardware. Software profiling is essentially the translation of library policies and procedures into machine form. For example, overdue procedures such as fine structures and billing dates must be programmed into the software. Other decisions such as which fields will be displayed in the various software modules must be made. Indexes and other access points must be chosen. Screen displays need to be designed. The involvement of the system administrator in this phase of planning will pay dividends later, especially in the ongoing maintenance and operation of the system and in the training of patrons and staff.

The duties of the system administrator can vary greatly within different libraries. In general the system administrator is responsible for the overall welfare of the system itself and for providing assistance to others who need to use the system. Once the hardware and software are installed and fully functional, the primary responsibility of the system administrator becomes system maintenance. This can be as mundane as cleaning tape drive heads and terminal screens, or as rare as troubleshooting a defective disk drive. Much of the routine maintenance and operations can be handled by support staff, if such assistance is available, and not by the system administrator. If the library computer is housed in a campus computer center, many routine functions can be taken over by its staff. For example, backup filesaves, whether daily or weekly, can be integrated into the workflow of the computer center. This frees the library staff of this time-consuming chore. These individuals are usually intimately familiar with the correct protocols of tape handling and storage. By keeping the library's backup tapes in storage, especially if a vault is available, with other campus tapes, a single reliable source for recovery is provided in the unlikely event of a catastrophic failure of computing equipment. In addition, the computer center will almost always have staff available to monitor the computer consoles. This can be beneficial if and when trouble arises. An integrated computing facility also provides ready access to other computing professionals on campus. These individuals can be an important source of information and assistance.

In addition to hardware maintenance, software maintenance is another major duty of the system administrator. As library policies and procedures change, it may be necessary to update the software configuration. For example, simple changes such as increasing the fines charged for overdues may be easily done locally by the system administrator. Other changes, such as the fields that are indexed or displayed, may require vendor assistance in order to alter the software itself. Software upgrades may provide the greatest challenges to the system administrator, especially if major changes have been made. For example, screen displays may be radically altered and commands may be changed. Such changes will require retraining of both staff and patrons. The installation of new software modules entails profiling and often requires hardware enhancements, in addition to training.

Troubleshooting of problems, whether hardware or software, may be one of the most difficult tasks of the system administrator. Everything from balky multiplexors, to tape drive errors, to software inaccuracies may perplex and exasperate him or her. Trying to decipher the problem requires a logical process, a thorough knowledge of the system, and a bit of educated guesswork. During such times the knowledge of the system administrator and his relationships with the vendor and other members of the library or college staff can be sorely tested. A sense of humor coupled with a desire to fix the problem will enable the system administrator to work the extra hours required to follow many dead-end leads. For example, among the most baffling of problems can be those related to telecommunications, since the source of the reported problem could lie in the user's or the library's modems, software, cables, computers, ports, telephone lines, the campus telephone switch, or even in atmospheric or astronomical conditions. One call into the system may fail, while the next may succeed. Isolating the source of the problem can, as a result, require many hours, if not days. During this time, the system administrator must often neglect his other duties, such as staffing the reference desk. This, in turn, places a greater burden on the rest of the staff.

Since the system administrator will generally have the most in-depth knowledge of the system's operation, he or she will often be called upon to answer specific questions both from the library staff and from patrons. Thus, assisting in the training of both staff and patrons becomes a priority. This training can vary from simple requests by patrons for instruction on logging onto the system from a home computer to helping the technical services staff decipher complex directions in vendor documentation for changing specific parameters such as default collection codes. Keeping current with documentation changes and updates must be a priority. To assist both patrons and staff, the system administrator should be knowledgeable about all phases of the system and be able to converse in layman's terms about it. Either writing or helping others write user documentation, especially the checking for accuracy of the information given, can also become a part of his or her duties.

Finally, serving as a central information source about the system is a major responsibility of the system administrator. This is often not considered until questions such as capability, use, vendor response, or integration into other campus networks, arise. The system administrator must often field many questions from other libraries which are investigating the chosen vendor for their own automation. Serving on campus committees that oversee computing can also be required. This can lead to contacts with others on campus who can share their expertise in computer matters. Alliances can be forged with these individuals which may result in stronger support for the library among both faculty and administration. Of special concern is maintaining good working relationships with the director of computing and with the administrators who control computing budgets. The library system administrator must often, as a result, become mired in campus politics.

Advantages of choosing a current public services librarian who has been involved with automation planning from the very beginning of the project as system administrator include a knowledge of the system itself; a complete understanding of the software, hardware, and configuration; a recognition of the needs and abilities of library users, both staff and patrons; and being a known entity on campus, one who is familiar with the institution, its mission, its limitations, and its financial condition. Most important is the recognition of the needs of users. Library systems should enhance access to information desired by patrons. Thus, a knowledge of how patrons use the library can assist in designing and profiling the software, the physical arrangement of terminals, and the selection of access points to the collection.

Disadvantages of choosing a public services librarian, while not outweighing the advantages, must be considered. These include the time it takes to learn a system thoroughly, especially if automation or computer experience is lacking; the lack of available library personnel with appropriate background or desire to fulfill the duties of system administrator; and Murphy's law, namely that system trouble will occur at the least opportune times, for example, at the busiest reference period when the system administrator will be taken away from tasks such as staffing the reference desk or doing bibliographic instruction. During the planning and implementation phases of the automation project, a great deal of time may be spent by the system administrator away from regularly assigned duties. After the system is fully operational, however, less time will be required for the effective management of the system except when problems arise.

In conclusion, the system administrator must possess a comprehensive knowledge of his library and its patrons. This knowledge should always drive decisions concerning the system, its configuration, and its operation. In some cases, several individuals on the professional staff of the library may be more than qualified to assume the duties of system administrator. A public services staff member, especially one who has a good working relationship with the technical services staff, may make a good choice to be system administrator. Knowledge of the user population is as important as knowledge of the system. The public services staff often knows the patrons better than others within the library. Library automation must be aimed at the user and not only at the staff, because the users are the ones who must be served. By involving the public services staff, especially the one who will become system administrator, in the entire automation project, a better system geared to the needs of patrons will result. The concept of service must remain paramount in both the design and implementation of the library system.

The key criterion for a successful system administrator is that of flexibility, because the system will often dictate what and when changes must be made. In addition, curiosity and the desire to learn about the system in detail and to probe into its inner workings will serve the system administrator and the library well.

ONE ALD FOR BOTH READER AND TECHNICAL SERVICES: A NEW ORGANIZATIONAL MODEL FOR ADMINISTRATION

Frieda M. Davison, San Francisco State University

When looking at classified advertisements in current library trade journals, one sees numerous positions for "holistic", "compleat" and even "renaissance" librarians. All of these words are being used to describe a concept which is making a return to the library profession. Specialists are diminishing. Generalists are once again being sought. Theoretically, librarians participating in these positions report to more than one person depending upon the functions and projects in which they are involved. Almost all include boundary-spanning responsibilities or responsibilities which cross traditional departmental lines. For example, a "compleat" librarian may catalog as well as staff a reference desk; may catalog as well as perform online bibliographic searches; may staff multiple service desks as well as perform collection development tasks; or may very well perform all of the above. There seems to be no parameters in the types of libraries seeking this "new" breed of librarians. Be they public, academic, special, small, large, private or government, there appear to be no restrictions.

This phenomenon is only one of the indications of reorganization that has become rampant in all types and sizes of libraries. What is causing this process of constant change and analysis in our once traditionally stable, comfortable and "stressless" profession? A quick look at the professional literature illustrates that these drastic changes began in the mid-1970s with the introduction of OCLC into technical services operations. Brian Alley gives a succinct account of these early changes in his article "Reshaping Technical Services for Effective Staff Utilization." (Ref. 1) In the late 1970s and early 1980s, several notables, including Michael Gorman, contended that technical services would become an extinct entity and some began implementing organizational structures which they felt would achieve that end. (Ref. 2) Several years later, in 1985, the Association of Research Libraries (ARL) published its SPEC Kit #112--<u>Automation and Reorganization of Technical and Public Services</u>. (Ref. 3) Depending on whose point of view one accepts, this report proves that either great strides are being made in tearing down perceived walls between the two areas and the profession is moving towards full integration <u>or</u> very little change is occurring and traditional lines of demarcation will remain in place for generations to come.

Since the publication of this report there have been numerous workshops, seminars, meetings, symposia and conferences devoted to this topic. For example programs and conferences have been sponsored by the Medical Library Association, the California Library Association, and the American Society of Information Science. The Midwest Academic Library Conference sponsored a two and one-half day institute in 1987 that addressed the topic of the holistic librarian. During the ensuing years since Gorman's prediction of the demise of technical services there has been a slow but steady migration towards integration rather than extinction.

While there has been steady migration towards integration of functions, tasks, files, etc., very little attention has been given to the attending changes that are required to manage and administer these new configurations. What is just now beginning to emerge is the recognition that upper level administrators must also be holistic or compleat.

Ann Prentice was among the first to acknowledge that we administrators are a major problem and present one of the largest stumbling blocks to creative and innovative operations in today's libraries. In her article, "Jobs and Changes in the Technological Age," Prentice notes:

"Managers who resist changes that technology may make on their work style may be very willing to enforce changes on others. They may not have an adequate understanding of the change technology makes and be unsympathetic to the concerns of workers. The majority of the top level managers are older, well-educated males--those who are most threatened by changes in the workplace. They are aware of the need to become technologically sophisticated but are often slow to function in the changing environment while at the same time insisting that their staff do so." (Ref. 4)

It is important at this point to clarify some terminology for the remainder of this paper. The uppermost level of administration and management being referred to by this paper is that of "library director." That term encompasses university librarian, library dean, director of library services, etc. The second level of administration this paper refers to is the assistant library director or the ALD. It encompasses terms such as associate library director, assistant or associate university librarian.

A few libraries have been able to grow towards integration at the ALD level. One of those is the University of Tulsa at Tulsa, Oklahoma. Integration of tasks and implementation of boundary-spanning responsibilities there led to re-organization in all units of the McFarlin Library. Consequently, there was also recognition that a new and innovative administrative structure would be required for the new functional organizational structure to succeed. As of June 1988, the new structure became effective whereby there is an Associate Director for General Services. This model places all operational units, including Special Collections, Technical Services, Public Services and Collection Development under one person--currently Mr. Donald R. Smith. (Ref. 5)

Unfortunately, most libraries do not have or do not recognize that they have in-house talent to accomplish integration at the upper levels of management. Remember the quote from Ann Prentice. San Francisco State University (SFSU) was one of the first university libraries in the nation to advertise for and hire in a combined position of Assistant Library Director for Reader and Technical Services.

The decision to combine positions of ALD for Reader Services and ALD for Technical Services was precipitated by several factors: (1) the implementation of an integrated library system was imminent with the installation of both an OPAC and a circulation module scheduled simultaneously; (2) long term senior library faculty were entrenched with little to no turnover anticipated for at least five years; (3) both ALD positions were vacant; and (4) severe budget cuts were being predicted. The final decision to combine the two positions was made by Library Director Olive James but had been recommended to her by the Library Council which is made up of representatives from every operational unit in the library.

By having both Technical Services and Reader Services report to one individual, it was hoped that several issues could be addressed and several objectives could be achieved. Among the most urgent were: (1) a joint effort by the two divisions to identify and achieve library-wide goals and objectives (such as increased automation throughout the library); (2) a deeper understanding and dove-tailing of division and individual unit-wide objectives, priorities and operations; (3) increased communication within the combined division specifically and throughout the library generally.

Making the decision, however, was probably the easy part. The first real challenge came in trying to identify qualifications for the position. Both Reader Services and Technical Services personnel felt prior experience in their respective areas was necessary. Management personnel were looking for candidates who also had some systems and/or OPAC experience. With these major qualifications, reality began to set in when a full search was completed and no one was satisfied with the prospects. One candidate even expressed his opinion during a onsite interview that the proposed merger was foolish and was sure to fail. Most library personnel now agree that that candidate was most interested in enjoying the sights of San Francisco!

A second search was completed during the summer of 1989. Yours truly was "unofficially" offered the position in late August pending the approval of university administration. Due to a variety of unprecedented glitches, paperwork was delayed in a Vice President's office and the "official" appointment approval was finally made the first week of October, 1989. Agreement was reached between the interested parties that the new ALD would begin January 2, 1990 with the primary objective of merging the two divisions as soon as possible.

On October 19, 1989 at 5:04 p.m., Mother Nature decided that she was going to be in charge of reorganization. The Loma Prieta seismic surprise struck the San Francisco Bay Area with forces not felt since 1906. University buildings were shaken and wrenched. Library personnel evacuated over 900 people and no one was injured. When inspectors re-entered the library, they faced a series of unbelievable sights. Asbestos had been shaken loose on two floors. Shelving had become a series of parallelograms which then toppled like dominoes. Microfiche and film were thrown from their drawers and then empty cabinets toppled. Approximately two thirds of our 1.2 million items landed on the floor.

November and December was spent learning about FEMA restrictions, allowances and required documentation; watching construction engineers invade the library with masks and tools of all shapes and sizes; watching "professional" movers stack volumes on top of one another (sometimes to heights in excess of four feet); and watching students line up at the glass doors peering in at the destruction.

Once library personnel were allowed entry into parts of the building, some emergency services were re-instituted. Around November 1, the Reserve Book Room was re-opened, telephone reference began, and paging for faculty research and classes began within stack areas that could be entered. All library personnel were utilized in a variety of recovery efforts--from identifying damaged materials to drawing floorplans for new stack configurations. Thus, the library that the new ALD entered on January 2, 1990 held a myriad of different problems, priorities and objectives than it had when she had taken the position three months earlier.

It is now approximately eighteen months later. The initial tasks facing the new ALD were very different than those anticipated but in an ironic twist these tasks contributed to a successful merger of the two divisions. The earthquake and recovery fostered a new comradery among library personnel. They had to rely on each other for safety, emotional support and physical strength. To many, merging Reader and Technical Services seemed less than challenging after all they had accomplished. From a management viewpoint, it was still a challenge but one which was easier because of the trust and understanding that had been fostered from the depths of disaster and emergency.

Let us now assess the current situation. There are weekly meetings of all unit heads reporting to the ALD. Each participant reports on events, concerns and progress within his/her respective unit. This has brought about a recognition that small unit decisions will most likely impact many library operations and personnel. The OPAC is now operational, even though there seem to be more problems with it than anyone anticipated. There is a general recognition and understanding that many of our OPAC problems result from the combined implications of being part of a large statewide bureaucratic system and having to accept the lowest bid in response to an RFP, rather than being in-house problems. We have conducted two one-half day retreats in which personnel at all levels in the combined division participated in identifying priorities for the coming year. Personnel in all units are staffing patron service desks. Planning and analysis are underway for adding an acquisitions module to the integrated system within the next year. Position descriptions are being rewritten to incorporate new tasks for a post-OPAC environment. As positions become vacant, each one is analyzed in terms of its contribution to the overall goals of the library and the priorities of the division.

Has the merger succeeded? We feel it has. Understanding has deepened. A reference coordinator recently told the bibliographic control coordinator, "I feel like I have an arm missing when you can't be at our meeting." A cataloger was the one who developed simple wording for the patron help screens on the OPAC. Catalogers and bibliographic processing staff routinely work on the information desk which provides support to the public OPAC terminals. Every person in the library is recognizing the impact of the integrated system and the need for multiple communication paths.

The coming year will undoubtedly offer more challenges to the once new ALD. University enrollment has increased dramatically over the past few years and is expected to increase again or at best remain the same. Unprecedented budget cuts are predicted for 1991/92. There will no doubt be a personnel budget freeze and layoffs are a possibility. Some units such as Special Collections, Maps, and Binding remain in at least a partial earthquake recovery mode. Continued progress must be achieved towards full implementation of an integrated library system. New services will no doubt be demanded by our very vocal students and faculty. Regardless of these "new" challenges, the underlying duties and responsibilities of the ALD will remain the same: To listen, to analyze, to guide, to review, to lead, to identify individual and group strengths and weaknesses, and to voice those attributes to the participants and the director in such a way that they will encourage creative thinking and innovative problem solving and will utilize each person's talents to the fullest.

In closing, I hasten to add that one ALD for both areas is not the answer for all libraries. However, it is an alternative which deserves serious analysis and consideration. It embraces the idea of "flattening" the hierarchical structure of the traditional library organization. It relieves the director of one level of analysis and decision-making which provides time for fund-raising or other time pressing activities. It is a challenging and rewarding experience for the incumbent. Jennifer Cargill recently wrote, "Without vision and the courage to change, libraries and librarians will find themselves on the sidelines." (Ref. 6) With that vision and courage to which Cargill alludes, the ALDs could very well become the quarterbacks that those other librarians watch from the sidelines!

1. Alley, Brian. Reshaping Technical Services for Effective Staff Utilization. Journal of Library Administration 9, No. 1, p. 105-110, 1988.

2. Gorman, Michael. On Doing Away With Technical Services Departments. American Libraries 10, p. 435-437, July/August 1979.

3. Association of Research Libraries. Automation and Reorganization of Technical and Public Services. SPEC Kit 112, 1985.

4. Prentice, Ann. Jobs and Changes in the Technical Age. Journal of Library Administration 13, No. 1/2, p. 47-58, 1990.

5. Smith, Donald R. Holistic Change in Academic Libraries. (unpublished position paper), University of Tulsa, 1989.

6. Cargill, Jennifer. Integrating Public and Technical Services Staffs to Implement the New Mission of Libraries. Journal of Library Administration 10, No. 4, p. 21-31, 1989.

LIBRARY FIELD TRIALS AND THE SOLUTION TO PROBLEMS OF INFORMATION RETRIEVAL IN THE LARGE

Horace Dediu and S.C. Chang, GTE Laboratories, Incorporated

ABSTRACT

An experimental information retrieval system has been ported to and tested in a library environment operating on a large number of large textbases. The systems environment consists of a heterogeneous, distributed hardware and software network. The data environment includes more than 30 distributed textbases whose total size is on the order of one Gigabyte. The user environment is a diverse user population of several hundred research, management and technical staff. We will present results from data conversion, usage, indexing and distributed retrieval experiments. We will also describe the new research issues that these experiments evidenced. In the environment just described, solving the information storage and retrieval problem requires the use of three hardware resources: storage, computation, and communication. These resources must be applied effectively to four information operations: conversion, indexing, retrieval and maintenance. For large, distributed systems, a near-optimal allocation of the three resources is necessary to maintain temporal information and to sustain throughput to the user.

1. Introduction

The evolution of an experimental system through research, development and implementation involves many iterations of feedback, refinement and sometimes re-thinking. The evolution of such a system (FAIRS) is the topic of this paper. In particular we are concerned with the problems of IR when the retrieval engine is stressed with several loads: size of the input, size of the user population, and the multitude and distribution of platforms (portability). Although not usually considered a topic for research, the study of the implementation of this IR system "in the large" has generated new research questions. The experience gained in generating, converting, indexing and using new databases has provided feedback to the research project and has, in some cases, taught us lessons, in others, confirmed that we are on the right path.

Here by "large" we mean that the system is being used with more than 30 textbases, with a total data size greater than 1GB, and a user population greater than 200. It is also of interest to note the rate of increase of all these quantities. Although bursty, we observed a linear rate of growth in the data size (both number of textbases and the total text size). Based on previous behavior, we assume that the size growth will continue to be linear. This basic assumption is consistent with our design of the IR system. Another assumption is that the environment (and hence the user population) in which FAIRS will run is a distributed, loosely coupled, coarse grained, heterogeneous network. We think such an environment typifies the modern information world. We also believe that such an environment is most likely to remain the model of future information systems. This paper will describe the implementation of FAIRS, the results of experiments with FAIRS on large data in a network, and the questions that arose from these results.

1.1. FAIRS

FAIRS (Friendly Adaptable Information Retrieval System) is a prototype information retrieval system developed at GTE Laboratories. It has evolved from a research project experiment to the core retrieval engine for a corporate distributed information network. FAIRS is unique among IR systems in its adoption of an open and adaptable ranking strategy. The system provides effective relevance feedback to the user and allows user interaction in working toward a perfect ranking. FAIRS uses free association for query interpretation instead of Boolean operators. It recognizes a negative dictionary, and a synonym list. The stemming process is fairly extensive in eliminating suffixes while prefixes are untouched. Fast retrievals are accomplished via full inversion.

FAIRS has an open approach to data formatting which minimizes the requirement for file conversion before indexing. FAIRS is portable across a large number of systems and is usable in a distributed environment. It uses standards such as ANSI control of character–based displays and the X Window protocol for graphics displays. FAIRS has links to OCR software for text input and scanner drivers for image grabbing. The retrieval process can return non–textual information categorized as multimedia. Images are handled in standard TIFF formats. Plans for enhancement include the addition of multimedia retrieval, query correction and automated information retrieval. FAIRS runs on PC's, UNIX, and VMS. It is written in Prolog and C.

1.2. The Information

We recognized early that the most appropriate Beta site for FAIRS testing was a library. The GTE Laboratories Library is a corporate information center as well as a technical research library. The prevalent data is the card catalog maintained as full text (>4MB). This data existed before FAIRS was installed and was being searched using the SIRE system [7].

The library catalog has since been converted to FAIRS. Since FAIRS was installed, more than 30 other textbases were added with minimal or no conversion. The most demanding data was Current Contents information collected as full text from the Institute for Scientific Information. That data set grows at the rate of approximately 2MB of text per week. Other information includes technical source documents, manuals, reports, reviews, catalogs, and all library holdings. The retrieval process has been linked to database applications such as circulation and routing. The description of these custom links are not in the scope of this paper, but the presence of links illustrates the flexibility of an open retrieval engine.

Also since the installation of FAIRS, other libraries have joined the Laboratories to form a network. The portability of FAIRS allowed a smooth transition. The new sites form an extension to the local network that in abstract terms is not a novelty. However, in physical terms, the extension is a leap in information sharing and transfer.

We ran experiments with large data sizes and determined which resource is likely to be scarce with such a load.

1.3. The Users

The system is accessed locally (using the local Ethernet backbone) and remotely, (Internet, DECNET, Telenet, modem). Because of such a wide user population we cannot give statistics on all users. Locally, however, the population consists of 650 technical and support staff, about 200 of which are frequent users (at least once per month). The users are mostly well versed in computer interaction. The number of local users will remain constant, but the number of remote users is likely to grow.

Although it's easy to count users, it's another thing to weigh their satisfaction. Our experiments in this area were of two types: The experiments on and with users involved the ease of operation (quality) in terms of time to reach satisfactory results, and their observations. The user load (quantity) on the system as a function of FAIRS throughput was also monitored.

1.4. The Platforms

Systems issues are seldom discussed in IR research. However, we found that to make an IR system usable, the platform system architecture should be a major concern. As temporal and unpleasant as it seems, a poor choice of platforms can make any elegant system appear clumsy and inefficient. A network composed of retrieval nodes and storage servers is well suited to distributed IR.

1.4.1. The Nodes

The physical port of FAIRS is onto a multi-user, multi-tasking distributed architecture. The network services are provided by variations of the UNIX operating system and the TCP/IP. User access is transparent and interactive. The hardware is VAX/Ultrix, VAX/VMS or Sun/SunOS. The user interface is best accommodated and had the highest throughput from X-Window servers. Other optional output is to any PC displays, VT-100 terminals and compatible ANSI terminals. It is difficult to explain the network topology since it is amorphous by design. Fortunately, FAIRS thrives in such an environment.

1.4.2. Storage

The target information is stored on large capacity disk systems. Some systems are optical, others magnetic. Some storage is temporary and used for indexing, other storage is archival and is used for retrieving.

2. Experiments and Results

The porting and physical installation of FAIRS was followed by its release to the user population. Predictably, we've had some reluctance to the new system from users and we encountered some problems. These problems can be classified into four categories: The *administration*, i.e. maintaining large text files and indexes, appending and updating temporal information. *Conversion*, i.e. generating text and converting text from other electronic formats. *Resource Allocation*, the classic problem in distributed systems. Finally, (and most importantly,) *usage*—the user's satisfaction with the quality of the system and the contents of the information base.

2.1. Administration

With Gigabyte textbases, new problems arise with the handling of data. In general, these are system problems, but systems have limits, and the IR engine should be able to adapt to those limits. The suite of IR mechanisms has to be split into parts which maximize resource sharing across a network. This meant distributing FAIRS across three categories of network nodes: Storage servers, Index servers, and Communication or retrieval servers. Since the indexing of large textbases requires many hours of disk-access intensive usage, the index task should be separated from the retrieval task, as it is response-time sensitive. Issues such as redundant or multiple indexing, backup and integrity maintenance also arise. Multiple indexing of the same data with different record sizes also had to be performed.

2.1.1. Indexing

Inevitably, some indexing (file inversion) jobs did crash. These faults were mostly due to hardware failures. The indexing would proceed for several hours before terminating with some error code. These hours would be wasted since the indexing would have to be restarted from the beginning. One solution to this problem is to use hardware for fault tolerance. This means using redundant parallel indexing—starting two independent jobs on separate nodes with the same input. If one process fails, due to a malfunction, the other is still likely to complete. After the first fails, it must be restarted on the assumption that the first instance of the second job will fail. This overlapped parallel approach is likely to succeed eventually. The concept can be extended as far as resources (number of CPU's available) allow. Redundant, overlapping parallel indexing is a thorough but expensive solution.

The drawback of implementing parallel indexing is the possible scarcity of hardware resources. If that is the case, the index program must be changed to create intermediary indexes which are saved to disk. Thus the indexing can be restarted at the last update. This solution is the most cost effective.

The indexing of large files can run into yet another problem: too many records. If the record counter is a variable of 8 bits, then the maximum record count is 256. If the variable is 16 bits, then the maximum record count is 32,768. On a 32-bit system the limit is 2,147,483,648 records—over 2 billion. This number seems large, but it may be too small in the future. The index program needs to have an open ended, infinite record count to be usable in the large.

2.1.2. Maintenance

The indexing paradigm used for FAIRS has the property that appending records is inexpensive in time, but deletion or modification (deletion followed by addition) is very expensive in time (a new index must be generated). If the data is being generated rapidly, (on the order of 10MB per week), indexing can be accommodated with current technology. If the data is being modified frequently, the system is inefficient. Thus, we use the system only for retrieval of archive type data. With any such archive, periodic maintenance is still necessary.

A compromise method is the periodic deletion of contiguous record blocks. The idea is as follows: For every file of text added, the oldest file is deleted from the text base and the index is automatically updated. This is done through a modification to the file inversion algorithm. The running time is not excessive and therefore the method is effective in keeping information current without re-indexing.

Maintenance consists of regular appending and infrequent modification of the archive. The appending can be done automatically and is usually a batch process. Editing is mostly done to remove duplicate records or to correct errors, or to remove old or obsolete information. Since the data is stored as text, the editing is actually done by a text editor. To edit Gigabyte files, the editor must be capable of working with very large files. We found the GNU Emacs editor capable enough on UNIX systems.

Another consideration is disk space. In general, the storage required for one unit of data is 1.5 units of index. We recommend that for a certain data size, 3 times that size should be available before the data is installed.

2.2. Building the Data

In generating the textbases, our experience has been both with the conversion from paper to full-text and from other electronic data to full-text. Among the formats we have converted are: Typeset text on paper; typed text on paper; word processing documents from various word processors on Macintosh, PC, VMS and UNIX; Macintosh database files; CD ROM files; IBM mainframe files in EBCDIC from magtape; and information downloaded through modem.

The philosophy of "using information as-is" was put to the test with every new textbase added. The conversions were generally easy and fast—small global changes to the text were all that was required. Data from Reflex Database on the Macintosh, Interleaf documents, PC files, and Word files were are handled with ease.

The Current Contents database arrives in an IBM mainframe/COBOL format on magnetic tape. The extraction of that data was accomplished with UNIX text processing tools and one program developed in-house. In general, we try to avoid any manual editing of the files, however, in some instances, the cost of manual modification is less than the cost of generating an automatic conversion method. The advantage of automatic conversion is the generation of conversion programs libraries which can be re-used.

We've also addressed the issues of re-formatting of text for aesthetics and compression or redundancy elimination. The Current Contents database originally arrives with 400% redundancy. We eliminated this and formatted it for readability.

Building electronic data from information is being done either by direct generation (manual entry, collection of electronic records into files, and optical character recognition) or by automatic conversion from electronic format to full-text.

2.2.1. Generation

The generation process for very large data sets must be done automatically for it to be efficient. We recommend downloading on-line information, using CD ROM, scanning and OCR before manual data entry. Using the first two methods, a rate of generation of 2MB/person-year can be sustained. This number varies greatly and is probably an underestimate. The OCR method is the fastest (up to 100MB/person-year), but most expensive in equipment, and the least flexible. For the one Gigabyte of data in its archives, the GTEL Library was responsible for only 1-2 MB of manual data entry.

In another experiment, documents which existed only in paper form were scanned, their images compressed, stored, and processed with OCR software, generating searchable text files. The entire process is automatic and has accumulated 300MB of images and text.

2.2.2. Conversion

The highest rate of growth for building data is achieved through data conversion. This growth rate is only limited by machine speed, availability and the rate of data gathering. The rate of 1GB/year is easily sustained. Non-encrypted data can be decoded and converted in time linear to data size. The automatic conversion process requires some programming effort, however. It can be shown that this time is quite easily bounded.

2.3. Resource Allocation

In a distributed environment there are multiple users on multiple hosts. Any one host does not have the capacity to sustain all tasks for all users, but the multitude can. We use a model of the IR network defined as a collection of three hardware resources: Storage, computation, and communication. These resources are distributed onto nodes, i.e. storage nodes, computation (indexing) nodes, and communication nodes. These resources must be applied effectively to four information operations: conversion, indexing, retrieval, and maintenance. Our problem is one of mapping the operations onto the nodes to maximize user satisfaction. We define user satisfaction (S) as the sum of the inverse of the response time to a query (R) plus the inverse of the difference between the time of availability of a data set to the administrator (A) minus the time of the availability of that set to the user (U).

$$S = \frac{1}{Response\,Time} + \frac{1}{Availability}$$

To minimize response time we must have a fast retrieval engine. In FAIRS the query interpretation, retrieval, ranking, and display of records is optimized to nearly constant time with respect to data size. We cannot improve R by much. The second variable in user satisfaction, the time of availability ($|U-A|$), can be improved by the judicious application of distributed computation. We chose to separate the conversion and indexing from the retrieval, while performing maintenance on yet another node. The transfer of data, location of data, and updating are not apparent to the general user. The method of distribution we used is not analytically derived and would be customized to each site. We used an empirical trial and error approach to solve the mapping problem.

2.4. Usage

The user responses to FAIRS have been mostly favorable. Those which were not favorable were not directed at FAIRS so much as to the IR approach in general. Why is this? This resistance was not so much from Labs' users, used to the SIRE full-text system, but from users familiar with database structures. The application of FAIRS to data not originally designed for full-text created a new and unfamiliar environment for its users. The concept of full-text retrieval was, and continues to be, mostly unfamiliar. The idea of finding information based on fuzzy queries and the ranking of retrieved objects contrasts with the structured, exact matching common in DB applications. Working with incomplete information is a task people perform habitually, but do not expect from a computer. The issue of no boolean operators has been very hotly contested by other librarians. There are many prejudices users have on how information should be retrieved. These prejudices were established by years of use of what we consider inadequate database systems for retrieval of archive information.

Our users are also those who convert or generate and administrate the system. The concept of record distinction came up with every new textbase introduced. The one and only syntactic structure a full-text retrieval system must know (or must have implied) is the boundary between records (or logical units). Often the conversion was not immediate, and some semantic mechanism was required to delimit the records. Contrary to the FAIRS philosophy, this required human intervention and processing.

The user interface is adequate but often confusing to those used to more complicated interfaces. Again, the experience in using databases works against the use of FAIRS. There are no fields, function keys, "screens", or hierarchical menus. Nor is there a thorough help feature (the FAIRS manual can be searched as full-text with corresponding images on-line). Regarding the character vs. graphical display debate. FAIRS is mostly character based, but can accommodate graphics interfaces, depending on the host platform. The interface issue has been dealt with by delegating its design to experts in the field. Rapid prototyping using Athena/MUSE is being pursued vigorously.

2.4.1. How to Find the Right Textbase

The proliferation of textbases has led to the meta-retrieval problem of selecting the right search set. Originally, a text-based flat menu system was used. Then we implemented a layered, hierarchical menu, which although sufficient, has limitations in usability. This deficiency went away with the development of X-window front ends. The "banner page" concept was used in at least one textbase as a "table of contents" feature. The banner page usually announces the name of the search set, but can also be used as a help screen and as a message-of-the-day type service. To solve the textbase search problem we propose another layer on the system with free search on the titles and descriptions of the textbases themselves. Such a layered retrieval may solve the problem, but we can't be sure yet.

2.4.2. DB/IR Practical Considerations

Embracing FAIRS has not led to the complete abandonment of database systems. We realize that the world is big enough for both technologies, but they should be applied appropriately for best results. As an example, the library maintains a database of circulation information which is queried and updated frequently. The DB approach is best applied here, and this will remain true even with future conversions. Similarly, journal routing and cataloging is strictly a DB domain problem. Both these databases are, and will continue to be, used with DBMS systems. The FAIRS book catalog system, however, does have a hook into the circulation system. In practice, DB and IR will be used simultaneously.

3. New Research Issues

IR in the large is quite different from IR in the small. Although the mechanism can be extended, new problems arise with sheer size. These problems have generated topics for further research:

The optimal mapping of IR operations onto IR resources on a distributed architecture. This is a problem which can be considered as subset of the more general optimal mapping problem, which is intractable. The lack of an analytical solution implies the need for heuristic solutions.

High speed indexing using parallel computation. Retrieval and ranking can be parallelized readily, but they are already fast enough for real-time. The indexing problem is more vexing. Its parallelization needs more research.

Automatic duplication removal and maintenance. With gigantic data sets, the maintenance task can become a full-time task for any human. Automatic detection of duplicates, misspellings and other errors should be corrected automatically. To this end, clever and fast spelling correction algorithms must be implemented.

Fault tolerance. The problem with indexing very large files has been discussed. Tolerating faults can be done in software or in hardware. Elegant software solutions must be found.

User interfaces for distributed IR. The user should not have to sense any distinction between retrieval of information stored locally or on the moon. IR systems should behave as information gathering agents (infobots) and present to the user relevant information quickly. This problem can also be classified with that of intelligent filtering and automated retrieval.

4. Conclusions

IR has shown itself to be an effective and increasingly promising technology for managing the information explosion. The technical difficulties are easier to surmount than the user's perceptions. Flexibility and openness are the most important virtues of an IR system destined for widespread real-world application.

5. References

1. Salton, F., McGill, M., *Introduction to Modern Information Retrieval*, McGraw–Hill, New York, NY, 1983.
2. Chang, S. C., Chow, A., Dediu, H., *FAIRS User's Manual*, GTE Laboratories, Incorporated, Waltham, MA, 1989.
3. Chang, S. C., Chen, W. C., "And–less Retrieval: Toward Perfect Ranking," *Proceedings of ASIS Annual Meeting 1987*, October, 1987, pp. 30–35.
4. Chow, A., Chang, S. C., *Text Structure Specification: A Study to Eliminate File Conversion*, Technical Note, GTE Laboratories, February 1988.
5. Chang, S. C., Chow, A., "Towards a Friendly Adaptable Information Retrieval System," *Proceedings of RIAO 88*, March 1988, pp. 172–182.
6. Du, M. W., Chang, S. C., Chow, A., "A2QDT: A Syntax–Directed Prolog Dialect Translator," *Proceedings of COMPSAC 89*, September, 1989, pp. 786–787.
7. Noreault, T., M. Koll, and M. J. McGill, "Automatic Ranked Output from Boolean Searches in SIRE," *Journal ASIS*, Nov. 1977, pp. 333–339.
8. Chang, S. C., Phuah, V., Dediu, H., Sasnett, R., "A Distributed Multimedia Information Retrieval System," *Proceedings of the International Conference on Multimedia Information Systems, 1991*, McGraw-Hill, Singapore, pp. 63–70.
9. Wolfman, S., Chang, S. C., "The Research Scientist as Sophisticated Library User: How has One Special Library Adjusted to the Emerging Sophisticated Information Needs?," *Proceedings of the 80th Annual Conference of the Special Libraries Association*," 1989, New York.

DLS MARC-UP: UPGRADING A CENTRALIZED ONLINE BIBLIOGRAPHIC DATABASE

Sandra R. Donahue, DuPage Library System

Keywords: Retrospective Conversion (Cataloging); Machine Readable Bibliographic Data; MARC System; OCLC, Inc.; DuPage Library System.

Abstract: DuPage Library System (DLS) is a cooperative organization of 28 public, 9 academic, 58 school and 28 special libraries serving over 735,000 people in Cook, DuPage, and Kane Counties in Illinois. Although the libraries remain independent, they share their materials and information through the use of a centralized online database which contains approximately 620,000 titles and 1,600,000 items. This database is maintained by decentralized data entry operations at the 16 online public libraries which constitute the DLS computer consortium.

Recognizing the need to improve communication proficiencies, expand searching capabilities, and facilitate integration with other electronic databases, the DLS Board of Directors adopted a Long Range Plan which incorporated upgrading the local database to full USMARC bibliographic format. Subsequently, a locally developed Request for Proposals was used to identify potential vendors to perform this service. Their written responses along with the outcome of a one thousand record sampling resulted in the selection of OCLC Conversion Services for batch processing via tape-to-tape machine matching, manual resolution of multiple matches, and manual disposition of non matches.

Search algorithms derived from the DLS electronic records were compared to the OCLC database and potential matches were verified for accuracy before being downloaded to magnetic tape for shipment to DLS. Approximately 339,000 records were processed through TAPECON Services, leaving 78,600 multiple matches for MICROCON*PRO and 76,500 non matches for RETROCON. Since September 5, 1989, the inputting of new records has been restricted to MARC formats and AACR2, level 2 cataloging standards.

The project was partially funded by a Library Services and Construction Act (LSCA) grant. The remainder was contributed by the sixteen online public libraries on a percentage basis determined by the size of their collection.

1. BACKGROUND

Today it is almost impossible to read a library publication attend a library conference, or even participate in informal discussion with other librarians without encountering the phrases "MARC format" or "MARC records." Nowhere is this more evident than in DuPage Library System (DLS) where a massive conversion project has been underway for the past three years. DLS is a Chicagoland cooperative organization consisting of 28 public, 9 academic, 58 school, and 28 special libraries serving over 735,000 people in parts of Cook, DuPage, and Kane Counties. Although the libraries remain independent, they share their materials and information through the use of a centralized online database which contains approximately 620,000 titles and 1,600,000 items. This database is maintained by decentralized data entry operations at the 16 online public libraries which constitute the DLS computer consortium.

2. VISION

Recognizing that MARC (an acronym derived from MAchine Readable Cataloging) has become the international standard for identifying, storing, and communicating bibliographic information, the DLS Board of Directors adopted a Long Range Plan of Service which addressed the need to upgrade the local electronic database to full USMARC bibliographic format.

2.1 Goals

The benefits of conversion were identified as follows:
Improvement of communication capabilities and resource sharing opportunities by adhering to standards;
Expansion of searching capabilities through unlimited number of fields and more precisely defined access points;
Provision for efficient interfacing of bibliographic records from preexisting databases as an alternative to original data entry;
Facilitation of offline accessory products such as CD-ROM and/or COM catalogs;
Increased database portability for bulk alterations and integration with preexisting databases.

3. FUNDING

When independent agencies are cooperating on an expensive undertaking, it is prudent to establish funding strategies before any controversial issues arise. DLS resolved this question an entire year before conversion began. Since the Illinois State Library had identified the standardization of databases as a funding priority in its Automation Long Range Plan (Ref.1), the project was partially funded by a Library Services and Construction Act (LSCA) Title I grant of $134,200. A major share of the cost, however, was absorbed by the sixteen online public libraries on a percentage basis determined by the size of their respective collections. The exact distribution is shown in the following chart.

3.1 MARC Assessment Chart

LIBRARY	TITLES HELD	% OF TOTAL	PORTION OF $200,000. DLS PAYS 1/17, ($11,756) LEAVING $188,235 TO BE SHARED BY LIBRARIES
Addison	72,952	6.411%	$12,067
Bensenville	60,089	5.280%	$ 9,940
Bloomingdale	39,939	3.510%	$ 6,607
Carol Stream	58,628	5.152%	$ 9,698
DuPage Library System			$11,765
Franklin Park	98,784	8.681%	$16,340
Geneva	61,969	5.446%	$10,251
Glen Ellyn	100,109	8.797%	$16,560
Glenside	43,973	3.864%	$ 7,274
Itasca	38,929	3.421%	$ 6,439
Naperville	136,952	12.035%	$22,654
Oak Brook	32,046	2.816%	$ 5,301
Poplar Creek	80,578	7.081%	$13,329
Roselle	51,395	4.516%	$ 8,502
St. Charles	109,286	9.604%	$18,078
Villa Park	101,482	8.918%	$16,787
Wood Dale	50,835	4.467%	$ 8,409
Totals	1,137,946	100.000%	$200,000

4. **VENDOR SELECTION**

Even though Illinois law does not require public agencies to solicit price quotations for computer services, the DLS Board of Directors determined that such an approach would be the best way to identify the appropriate MARC conversion vendor.

4.1 Request for Proposals

Administrators and technical services librarians from the online libraries devoted five months to collating a locally developed Request for Proposals (RFP). Adhering closely to the guidelines of Edwin M. Cortez (Ref.2), they included general and technical specifications and a detailed but flexible timetable. The final document was distributed to all potential candidates identified through advertisements in library publications and searches of library literature.

4.2 Evaluation

An evaluation committee was formed to review all responses to the DLS RFP. The team included two consortium library administrators, one DLS Board member, a technical services librarian, the DLS Executive Director and the DLS Automation consultant. No outside consultant was used on the project, but a great deal of unofficial advise was contributed by other Illinois library system automation coordinators, especially Mary Ann Atkins of Bur Oak Library System.

4.3 Criteria

Proposals were evaluated principally on the basis of the following criteria:
Compliance with specifications (or suggested acceptable alternatives);
Size and scope of the vendor's database;
Past experience and performance with similar projects;
Projected hit rate;
Delivery schedule;
Costs;
Ability to provide full USMARC records for all titles in the DLS database.

4.4 The Decision

Three finalists were required to provide, both in print and on nine-track tape, the processed results of a one thousand record sample chosen by the technical services librarians from the consortium libraries. The sample results were analyzed for hit rate, quality of MARC records, and percentage of erroneous matches. Based on the vendors' written responses to the RFP and the outcome of the sampling results, OCLC Conversion Services were chosen for machine matching of single hits and manual resolution of multiple and non matches.

5. PREPROCESSING

As a first step to converting the DLS machine readable database to MARC format, the local electronic records were copied to streamer tapes and sent to Auto-Graphics for downloading to nine-track tape. This option was chosen to expedite the process, adhere to established timelines and reduce the possibilities of errors.

The resulting tapes were shipped directly to SOLINET, the subcontractor designated for converting the data into search keys suitable for matching against OCLC's database. The primary match field was determined from the OCLC established order of preference as follows: OCLC control number, LCCN, ISBN, ISSN, CODEN, MPN, GDN, Personal-Name/Title, and Title. For verification purposes, search keys were qualified by format, date, and microform/not microform. Specific DLS information added to the search keys included the local author/title ten digit codes, local control numbers, and the owning libraries' symbols.

6. TAPECON

TAPECON service is a tape-to-tape batch processing service that upgrades machine-readable records to full USMARC format. Upon receipt of the SOLINET search keys, OCLC began a machine comparison against its own twenty-two million MARC record database. Each time a search key successfully matched a single record in the OCLC Online Union Catalog (OLUC), that record was downloaded to 9 track tape along with the merged local information.

A value added byproduct of the project was inclusion of the DLS three letter OCLC holding symbol on each OLUC record that was used which has expanded resource sharing capabilities nationwide. The number of OCLC interlibrary loan requests received at DLS has increased 10,000 percent! At the conclusion of TAPECON, a total of 339,221 single matches had been extracted for a hit rate of 68.63 percent. DLS incurred unit charges for successful matches only, and these included the price of the resulting tapes.

7. RETROCON

A specially designed TAPECON report was generated to facilitate the conversion of the 76,500 non matched records through OCLC's RETROCON Service. RETROCON is a customized program developed according to mutually agreed upon specifications between OCLC experienced catalogers and DLS technical services librarians. Trained OCLC staff members manually search OLUC in an attempt to find a matching record. When a match is encountered, local information and the DLS OCLC holding symbol are appended.

If no matching record is found, original MARC tagging is performed according to criteria established by technical services librarians from the consortium librarians. At the time of this writing, a total of 42,528 records have been processed through RETROCON. Since this is a labor intensive operation, completion is not expected before September 30, 1991.

8. MICROCON*PRO

The final phase of this project involves resolution of 78,500 multiple matches resulting from TAPECON processing. Three local database cleanup specialists began reviewing the customized exception reports for the two to ten hits in July of 1990, and by August they had already examined 33,535 of these records. However, DLS had hoped from the beginning that enough funding would be available to permit full USMARC inputting of unresolved titles by the vendor.

In December it was determined that MICROCON*PRO was indeed an affordable and cost effective way to complete MARC conversion. MICRO*PRO is a microcomputer-based, batch method of retrospective conversion whereby OCLC trained staff members inspect the exception reports, identify the correct record, and enter search keys and local data onto floppy disks. These search keys are then machine-matched against the OCLC online catalog and subsequent procedures are the same as for TAPECON. Contract negotiations for OCLC MICROCON*PRO services are currently underway; and December, 1991 has been targeted as a completion deadline.

9. CONCLUSIONS

DLS MARC-UP was not without its problems; that can always be expected with a major project. There were for example, several schedule setbacks. Because the Illinois State Library needed approval from the U.S. Department of Education before funding automation projects under Title I, federal monies were not available until six months into the conversion. Auto-Graphics experienced technical difficulties and failed to meet its downloading delivery timetable which affected the DLS queue position for SOLINET preprocessing. Finally, OCLC had not developed the computer programming needed to execute its original plan of a second TAPECON machine match with a revised search key, and vendor negotiations were delayed.

Wrong matches have been the source of considerable frustration to technical services librarians who have strived for a clean database for ten years and to circulation personnel who cannot determine which person has what materials charged out. A recent sample of one thousand converted records showed a four percent error rate which is almost exactly the same percentage rate indicated by the original sample. Four percent is low, but four percent of 500,000 records is still 20,000 different cleanup tasks.

On the positive side, three unexpected bonuses have already surfaced. First, online libraries have become more aware of the additional computer hours needed for MARC inputting and voted to purchase an uninterruptible power supply to prevent electrical power outages downtime. Second, administrators have realized that long range planning is needed to prevent the necessity of such massive conversion efforts in the future, and they have begun to formulate an automation strategic networking plan. And third, resource sharing activities have increased beyond all expectations, emphasizing the importance of expanding electronic access to information.

Therefore, DLS consortium libraries remain excited about retrospective conversion. They are looking forward to instituting a MARC based online public access catalog with enhanced searching capabilities through keyword and Boolean access. The benefits to DLS online libraries will be benefits to the entire library community. DuPage Library System is anticipating a day when there will be fast and easy access to information on a national level. This project is viewed as one small step toward reaching that vision.

10. EPILOGUE

To further increase retrieval capabilities, the DLS Board of Directors has recently established an auxiliary goal of applying authority control to its full USMARC bibliographic database. DLS will use the services of Blackwell North America, an acknowledged leader in the field, to match its bibliographic headings against a master file and upgrade its MARC format records to conform to Library of Congress practices and to generate a master file of authority records for ongoing control. The results of authority control processing will be replacement of applicable headings with current forms of entry, and creation of local authority records for headings not matched. Like MARC-UP, this project is also being partially funded by a Library Services and Construction Act (LSCA) Title I grant.

11. REFERENCES

1. Illinois State Library Automation Committee. "Plan for Funding Automated Resource Sharing in Illinois Libraries." _Illinois Libraries_, LXXI (March-April, 1989), pp. 218-236.

2. Cortez, Edwin M. _Proposals and Contracts for Library Automation: Guidelines for Preparing RFPs_ (Studio City, California: Pacific Information Incorporated, 1987), pp.1-69, _passim_.

EDUCATIONAL CONSTRUCTS FOR COMPUTER AND LIBRARY SCIENCE PERSONNEL

Charles D. Hurt, University of Arizonia

Keywords: Library Science, Computer Science, Engineering, Education, Academic Libraries, Special Libraries

Abstract: Integration of computer and library staff, especially in academic and special libraries, is increasing. With the increase in integration there is a concomitant increase in the desirability for educational programs which maximize aspects of both areas. A literature search was conducted over five years of literature in the computer science and engineering areas and in the library and information science areas relating to educational standards and requirements. Under the assumption that parallel or similar educational tracks will improve the working relationship between computer staff and systems librarians, an analysis was conducted to determine an optimal educational package for systems librarians and computer staff who work with library applications. A frequency weighting of concepts and methodologies in the literature for the last five years was used as a basis for using maximization techniques to determine the best mixture of course work for a systems librarian or a computer staff member who works with libraries. The convergence points of agreement were of particular interest as potential basic courses for concepts for joint curricula. The results of the study suggest that the differences may be more of a matter of emphasis than of actual substance but that library and information science is considerably more qualitative in approaching systems than is computer science or engineering. Of special note is the lack of standards, as the term is normally used, in library science education. This is a suggested as a damaging weakness in the educational process.

1. INTRODUCTION

The purpose of this study was to explore educational constructs in computer science, engineering, and library and information science for similarities. While such similarities may be of interest in general, the specific goal here was to use them as a basis for bridging the gap between computer science and library and information science. The phenomenon of integration of computer science staff and library science staff in academic libraries is a concern in the literature (Ref 1). This literature also suggests that there may be some semantic and conceptual difficulty in moving the two areas into closer proximity. One means to reduce the level of cognitive dissonance is to move the educational structures for the two areas into closer agreement.

One of the arguments for doing so at this point in time is that the American Library Association in currently reviewing their *Standards for Accreditation.* Both computer science and engineering have relatively stringent standards in place for their respective disciplines. If there is to be a melding or merger, there should be some attention paid to both content and semantics in moving library science and computer science, and, in some ways, engineering closer to one another. Not only would the educational enterprise benefit, but the specific professions and professionals would gain better understanding of each other's positions. For a discussion of the accreditation issue in library and information science, see the proceedings of ALISE/H.W. Wilson Foundation Accreditation Conference (Ref 2).

At the outset, this study did not approach the problem as one of a dearth of intellectual content in library and information science. The opinion here is that library and information science has a great deal to offer both computer science and engineering. The converse is also true. The mutual sharing of educational constructs should work to the benefit of each discipline.

The one area where this study begins from a negative stance is the issue of the *Standards for Accreditation.* Standards in computer science and in engineering have a very different connotation. Dictionary definitions of the term "standard" do not correspond to the practice of accreditation in library science. The emphasis here is on the positive, however. Accreditation can be a powerful tool, but it must clearly and unequivocally speak to quality and tests and measures of quality.

2. **METHODOLOGY**

The methodology used to explore the problem addressed here was to search the literature for the last five years in the three areas of library and information science, computer science, and engineering for publications which addressed the problem of educational constructs and curricula. The databases, LISA, COMPENDEX PLUS, and INSPEC were searched to develop the data for the study.

Material was scanned for the period in each of the three areas and a frequency count was made of terms in the literature. The data set then consisted of a database of word frequencies in each of the three areas. A threshold value was chosen to delimit the data sets. In all three cases, a limit of 50 occurrences was chosen as the boundary. This threshold was chosen not for any theoretically based reason but solely on the basis of examination of the raw data.

Following the frequency analysis of the various terms, a maximization technique which accounted for the frequency weighting of the terms in each of the three disciplines was utilized. The form of the maximization formula is as follows.

$$\max(x)$$
$$x = f(c)$$
$$50 < c < 484$$

where 50 is the threshold and 484 is the upper limit of the data set. C is the construct under examination.

The rationale for maximization was that it allowed the natural frequencies for each of the areas to operate and also allowed equal weighting across the three disciplines. There was no attempt to rank or weight any of the three disciplines higher than another. The goal was to determine, in theory, the optimum educational package for systems librarians and computer staff personnel working with library applications.

Specific attention was paid to the terms which were similar or appeared to be similar. While jargon and nuances often confound all but the most adept in a particular discipline, the occurrence of similar terms might be interpreted as evidence of similar educational constructs.

Library Science	Computer Science	Engineering
Literature	Programs	Systems
Information	Data	Analysis
Collection	Computation	Microcomputer
Communication	Databases	Software
Development	Management	Computer
Sources	Automation	Simulation
Microcomputer	Information	Information
Cataloging	Information Storage	Modeling

3. **RESULTS**

The results of the study indicated there is similarity than might first be presumed. The results do indicate there are substantial differences, to be sure. At the same time, the results also suggest strongly that there are significant areas of mutual interest. In some cases, the interest levels differ, suggesting a variance in terms of emphasis.

Two tables are given below. The first is a ranked list of the top twenty educational concepts in each of the three disciplines. The second is a table of terms in the literature which were combined using maximized frequency weighting.

Library Science	Computer Science	Engineering
Classification	Information Retrieval	Communication
Information Science	Communication	Research
Management	Processing	Automation
Research	Research	Expert Systems
Information Storage	Structures	Networks
Information Retrieval	Networks	Databases
Automation	Organization	Systems Analysis
Media	Artificial Intelligence	Human Factors
Organization	Software	Operations Research
Networks	Logic	Linear Systems
Databases	Mathematical	Artificial Intelligence
Policy	Design	Computation

Table 1
High Frequency Educational Constructs

Common Components
Systems
Organization
Microcomputers
Automation
Databases
Management
Communication
Networks

Common Components
Research
Information Storage
Information Retrieval
Software

Table 2
Maximized Frequency Weighted Constructs

4. CONCLUSIONS

The results of this study are considered very positive. They point out that, at least in terms of the literature discussing education and curricula, there is reasonable convergence in terms of educational constructs in the three areas. By no means is the convergence suggestive that one group is dominant. The variance in each of the three suggests that the three groups have different approaches to similar problems. The differences, in a number of cases, appear to be levels of emphasis as opposed to complete disparity. Library and information science appears to be more qualitative in its approach to the educational constructs. This is to be expected, especially when comparing library and information science to engineering.

The matter of library and information science being more qualitative in the approach to systems is not surprising and was expected. Qualitative is a relative term, however, as is quantitative. In this case there appears to be significant evaluative skills emphasized in library and information science and significant mathematical prowess expected of the engineer, and to a slightly lesser extent, the computer scientist. It should be noted that these are impressions which were not examined in the study.

5. DISCUSSION

As was noted in the introduction, one of the reasons for this study was to address the glaring lack of any standards in library and information science with respect to educational constructs. The present standards and the standards which are proposed do nothing to strengthen the profession and much to seriously harm it. Standards must be viewed as a quality-driven device for insuring excellence. The proposed standards in library and information science do none of this. They do not speak to the issues of educational excellence, nor do they map out definable quality programs. Computer science and engineering have addressed this problem and have arguably solved it. Library and information science has yet to address it and is unarguably a considerable distance from solving it.

One specific way engineering and computer science have addressed the quality argument is to require educational constructs – not courses necessarily – as a part of the accreditation process. Library and information science would be well served explore at greater length and depth the efficacy of this approach. Not only does it make intuitive sense, but it is successful in two other disciplines with which library and information science has felt some intellectual affinity. Additional work such as this to synthesize constructs will assist in this process.

This paper takes the position that the integration of computer staff and library staff is not only inevitable, but desirable. As this trend continues, the quality of the library and information science professional will be directly related to his or her academic preparation. This militates strongly against the overly technical and myopic training that the majority of students in library and information science programs receive. What these students need is education, not training. The question is, education to what end? This paper attempts to suggest some direction for this question. It is incomplete, but it is a beginning.

NOTES

1. Cimbala, Diane J. The Scholarly Information Center: An Organizational Model. *College and Research Libraries,* p. 393-398, September 1987.

2. Seavey, Charles A., ed. The ALISE / H. W. Wilson Foundation Accreditation Conference, September 16-18, 1984, Chicago, Illinois. Published in *Journal of Education for Library and Information Science.* 25, No. 2, p. 63-162, 1984.

SYSTEM MIGRATION: BETTERING TOMORROW TODAY

William Jacob, Norwalk Public Library

Keywords: System Migration, Database Migration, Compatibility, Stand-Alone, Network, Migration, Norwalk Public Library

Abstract: System migration is fundamental to library automated development. It is the primary method for a library to move from one system to another and from a first-time purchase to subsequent system purchases. System changeover commits a library to enhanced computer applications. It also commits a library to a complex and time-comsuming process. Thorough planning is essential for its success, especially database upgrade and migration to a new product. The Norwalk Public Library migrated to an integrated on-line system in 1990. It open a new era in Connecticut's library automation history. It was the state's first major public library to move from a network-based system to a stand-alone product. Its migration incorpoarte many common elements necessary for a successful system migration. This paper reports on the process of system migration in a network environment and Norwalk Public Library's experience in successfully changing systems.

SYSTEM MIGRATION: BETTERING TOMORROW TODAY

System migration is central to library automation. Today many libraries are facing the need to upgrade or replace their automated systems. They seek the advantages of emerging technologies at reduced costs. First and second generation systems are giving way to the latest products in the library automated marketplace. System migration is the evolutionary process that bridges one system to the next. It is an on-going process of renewal. It makes available the latest computer applications while addressing traditional information needs. System migration is a continuing process that reaffirms a library's automation commitment.

A library undertakes a system migration for improvement

or expansion of essential services. Affordable costs attract it to the benefits of today's technology. Expanded system capabilities secure its commitment to the automated product. A library's first automated purchase may emphasize a single function. Automating circulation activities once enabled it to lay claim to state-of-the-art technology. Today a library is drawn to integrated, multi-functional alternatives. It configures its automation future on the requirements that span a full host of library services. A library is conscious of the success or limitations of its present system and values its next purchase as a better investment.

The 1990s is a period of evolution in library automation. The latest computers are replacing yesterday's systems. Shifts from one vendor to another are becoming commonplace. Migrating a system champions library development. It is spurred on by new and improved applications in computer technology. The changing nature of on-line systems attracts libraries to a better product so as to expand and enrich services to its community.

On July 1, 1990 the Norwalk Public Library, Norwalk Connecticut, successfully migrated to an integrated, multi-functional on-line system. It completed a process of planning, selection and installation that stretched over twenty months. Norwalk became Connecticut's first major public library to move from a network-based system to a stand-alone setting and from proprietary to open technology. Presently, Norwalk is operating a fully integrated stand-alone system. Less than a year ago it was a member of Connecticut's largest private circulation consortium.

The Norwalk Public Library operates a main library facility and one branch, serving a municipal population of 80,000 in southwestern Connecticut. It maintains a multi-media collection of nearly a quarter of million items for public circulation. Its commitment to automation is strong and parallels generally what took place throughout the State of Connecticut during previous two decades.

A growing awareness of technology's value stimulated interest in computerizing library activities during the 1970s. Alternative forms of automation were analyzed and by the decade's end a decision took shape either to purchase a stand-alone system or become a founding member in a shared automated system. Cost advantages and resource sharing proved decisive. In 1980 Norwalk joined three other public libraries in a venture that would become the state's largest consortium to automate circulation activities. It remained an active member and customer of the regional grouping throughout the decade. By mid-1988, however, library staff were redefining Norwalk's automation future and the direction it would take.

Norwalk's decision to move to local system technology reflected similar concerns and goals of many migrating libraries. It questioned escalating vendor costs that supported outdated technology. It recognized substantial savings and service improvements that come with integrated library automation. On-line public access catalog, acquisitions, serials control, media booking and dial access combined with circulation maximized system performance at costs favorable to libraries.

System migration presupposes that an existing automated library system is in operation and requires replacement. It may consist of upgrading part or all of an automated system. This article defines a system migration as the total replacement of a library's automated system, consisting of at least a circulation module, either with its vendor's latest product line or a competitor's newest system. Key to any changeover is the transportability of a library's database from one product to another or from one vendor to its competitor.

At first glance changing systems seems no different than a library's first-time purchase. There is, in fact, a strong similarity between selection and implementation that procured the library's first system and its purchase of subsequent systems. The process includes many common elements. Planning, requests for proposal, bid evaluations, and vendor contract negotiations characterize both. System requirements, functionality, hardware configurations, vendor support, acceptance criteria, and reliability specifications also create the impression that system migration and system purchase are synonymous.

But a system migration is not a repeat of a library's original purchase. Changing systems introduces a new array of considerations missing from first-time planning. Migration of data files take on paramount importance. Initially, library concerns focused on moving from a manual environment to an automated setting. Planning structured building a database, usually for automated circulation activities. Second system planning requires meeting new system specifications and expanded system capabilities. Transporting database files avoid reconversion of circulation information. Upgrading brief records to full MARC format amplify system performance. System migration brings to a library the full value of the latest computer applications while laying down the process that will guide it through future system changeovers.

Changing systems is a costly and complex process, subject to risks and even failure. Careful planning is critical to its success. A well planned migration accelerates system implementation. It reduces delays, avoids disasters and economizes costs. Planning builds on staff strengths and library experience. It educates in areas of limited knowledge. Planning is a time-consuming commitment that rewards by minimizing risk and enhancing success.

In late 1988 Norwalk's Board of Directors committed the library staff to seek out an alternative to its present automation vendor, thus beginning the migration process. Cost, service and independence guided its decision. Four months later it selected a vendor of choice. Nearly a year of staff analysis and preparation supported their decisions.

For sometime library staff were aware of the dramatic shifts in the library automation marketplace. In the fall of 1987 the Library Director constituted an Automation Committee to investigate trends in technology and make recommendations on their application to library services. Later the charge was redefined to investigate, analyze and compare alternatives to the Library's current system. Preliminary reviews on stand-alone integrated systems took several directions. Literature reviews, conference attendance and workshops started the process. Site visits, vendor demonstrations and meeting with automation specialists accelerated it. Eventually, their summary evaluation produced a system recommendation that was endorsed by the Board of Directors.

Up to this point, the planning process was able to draw on staff experience. Under the direction of the Library Director and Project Administrator, their background and skills certified success throughout system selection. But migrating to a new vendor opened the planning process to many unknowns. Moreover, little help was available state-wide. None of Connecticut's public libraries had attempted a system changeover, especially from a private network.

How best to proceed was central to Norwalk's system migration. The Library's administrators were aware of the risks facing them. Migration opened new ground in Connecticut's library automation history. From the beginning they worked to identify and address areas of uncertainty. They sought guidance from legal and automation professionals. What initially seemed intimidating was analyzed and planned for step-by-step implementation.

Not until there was a selection of a system vendor could planning incorporate all elements of a system migration. System contract negotiations and installation, vendor upgrade work, site preparation and the funding converged into a plan of action. While each element was important, database migration proved the most difficult, the most time-consuming and riskiest. Its realization required intensive and thorough planning between the Library's Director and the Project Administrator.

Migrating a library's database distinguishes a system

migration from a first-time system purchase. Planning system configuration, system implementation and site preparation are common to both first and second-time purchases. Data files, however, create complications that are critical to the process of moving from a current product to its replacement. Transportability of bibliographic, patron and item records in a compatible format determines the level of success in a system changeover.

Machine-readable records are vital to the implementation of circulation and public access catalog functions. Brief circulation records place severe restrictions on an integrated automated system. They make meaningless many of the attributes of public access to an automated catalog through keyword and boolean searching. A library moving to an integrated system may own brief circulation records that require database preprocessing. Contracting a merge of short-form records with full MARC bibliographic records will be part of the migration process. Concomitant with an upgrade to full MARC format will be the removal of duplicate records and authority control of names and subject headings.

What tranfers from one system to another in a migrating a library's database will depend on vendor compatibility. Migrating to the same vendor's newest product supports ease of data transference in an acceptable form. Moving to a competitor's product creates problems due to differences in vendor operating systems. Software incompatibility may result in a library's failure to load its database without a customized loading program.

Underlying both bibliographic format and software compatibility is the library's ownership of its database. Ownership allows a library to migrate freely, to convert to MARC format at its convenience and to test database compatibility without hindrance. Lack of ownership greatly complicates database migration planning and system migration scheduling.

A system migration in a network environment poises concerns not found in a stand-alone setting. A stand-alone library maintains its database and may act independently in migrating to a new system. It can contract for conversion work on data it possesses without third party approval. Furthermore, moving from a stand-alone system allows the library to maintain its system if its scheduled start-up date is postponed.

A network library must obtain its data files from a shared database. It is dependent on procedures for network withdrawal and its mechanism for data extraction. Withdrawing from a network may require the termination of a service contract that may leave a library without automated operations if its on-line date is pushed back.

Nor are these the only differences that shape the process of a system changeover. A stand-alone library maintains a vendor relationship. It is primarily contractual and is continued or terminated on business reasons. Formal agreements also characterize network participation but there is an interdependency that links member libraries personally, financially and structurally. To leave a network includes reasons of not just cost and service but also direction and governance. Departure may be looked on as a threat to consortium viability and staff job security. Or it may be accepted as a library's opportunity to better service at lower costs. Co-operation can not be taken for granted. It is an on-going process that will require continuous reinforcement. What takes place during the data extraction process will reflect a level of co-operation proportional to a library's network relationship.

Network participation presented the most serious problem to Norwalk's system migration. Ownership of its database resided with its circulation vendor. Only through termination of its circulation contract and after a period of ninety days was the Library entitled to its data at an undefined charge. And then, only brief circulation records were available in an unspecified format. Furthermore, Norwalk's circulation vendor operated a proprietary computer system, limiting its ability to provide data compatible to any system Norwalk was likely to select as its replacement.

The nature of problems in database extraction required professional support and advice. Automation specialists worked with the Library's administrators in defining a process for the migration of the Library's data files. Once notification of contract termination was forwarded to the Library's network, library would begin negotiations for data extraction. It would contract with a database conversion vendor to upgrade the records to full MARC and authority control names and subject headings. The database vendor would insure compatibility of the processed database with the system selected by the Library. Finally, the City's Data Processing Center would convert extracted patron records for usage in the new system.

In quick succession the Library notified a database upgrade vendor of its selection and forwarded its network written notification of termination of its contract. At the same time other elements of the migration progressed rapidly. Contract negotiations went forward with a system vendor. Library administrators outlined a general plan for site renovation that included a computer room, installation of an uninterrupted power supply system, cabling and electrification of the Central and Branch buildings. Finally, the Library initiated talks with the City's Finance

Department for funding a system migration.

Time was now a special concern in migration planning. No longer was it an expendable commodity. A replacement system must be fully operation by a specific date or the Library would be without automated services. Early on the Library's administrators drew up time-lines for major elements in the migration. They mapped them to run parallel rather than sequentially to one another. They also factored a three month margin for delays into the process. Scheduling multiple time-lines with flexible converging points for completion reduced the dependency of one part of the migration on another. It also eliminated loss through elapse time among different phases of the changeover process.

Not all goes as planned. Delays and the unexpected may set back a migration by days or weeks. Work moves quickly wherever the library exerts influence. Time-lines chart progress, link converging work and margin extra time. But there are areas outside a library's control and subject it to unanticipated problems.

Norwalk experienced two deviations from its time-table. Each was important but not detrimental to the migration's success. Each was unanticipated and concealed its own reward.

The Computer Company, the Library's upgrade vendor went out of business shortly after completion of a contract. Months of work on database specifications, contract terms and city funding, vanished with a telephone call from its sales representative. The Library's system vendor calmed a tense situation by securing another upgrade vendor within twenty-four hours. But a new contract required negotiations and reintroduction into the City's funding process.

Even had The Computer Company remained in business, the Library lacked a database for it to upgrade. Negotiations with the Library's circulation vendor had stalled. An agreement on data specifications and tape format was reached but delivery would take an additional ninety days. The original plan in bringing together the Library's circulation records with an upgrade vendor was postponed by three months.

In the interim negotiations with its system vendor , who was brokering the upgrade contract, took a surprising turn. Shortly before Norwalk received its circulation database, its system vendor concluded the purchase of the library division of The Computer Company. Not only would Norwalk's original vendor perform its upgrade, but, as a division of its system vendor, it guaranteed Norwalk compatibility between its database and system. The delays consumed much of the extra time set aside, but the outcome assured Norwalk's successful migration.

System migration links a library's desire for bettering services to automation's rewards. It moves a library into tomorrow's computers today. Its benefits are immediate and translate into public support. An on-line public access catalog offers value to library patrons that is readily understood. Their response is instantaneous and overwhelming. It is spirited by a level of access that was never available in the controlled vocabulary of the card catalog.

Norwalk renewed its commitment to improving patron services by migrating to automation's latest product. Today an on-line catalog, powered by keyword and boolean capabilities, greet its patrons. New and old generations of library patrons are taking easily to library technology's most successful service. And more is in the offing. Expanded system services will open the Norwalk's "doors" 24 hours a day. Home access will permit dial-up services to its database day or night. Terminals will link the city's schools to its collection. Gateway services will give the library user expanded access beyond the its local resources. Norwalk is bettering tomorrow today.

FAREWELL TO TECHNOCRACY: A PUBLIC SERVICE MANIFESTO FOR THE ONLINE CATALOG

Lee Jaffe, University of California, Santa Cruz

SUMMARY

The library automation environment is changing and libraries need to change with it. In the past two decades we have seen an awe-inspiring parade of new technology enter the library. From the initial, tentative use of national online utilities and indexing services, to creating the first local online systems, first for processing and then for public access, and now CD-ROM services and supercatalogs, we have seen technology touch and change nearly everything that we do as librarians. And librarians have gained the expertise to go with the new systems.

However, with few exceptions, we have not made significant corresponding changes in the way libraries organize, manage or conduct themselves. For the most part, libraries follow the bureaucratic organizational model, which is better suited to control and stability than creativity and change. Within this model, responsibility for development of library technology is centralized. Whether this authority is called the "systems office" or the "center for knowledge enhancement," it is a technocracy, rule by technicians.

While the creation of a library technocracy was at best a expedient means of implementing new systems in the early days of automation, it is increasingly an impediment to innovation. The heart of this problem is that innovation always comes from the outside. From its isolated position, the systems office is not able to assess needs or design effective solutions that now face libraries.

Research on the development of technical applications shows that they fail most soundly when the designers ignore the culture and dynamics of the setting in which they are installed. In other words, those solutions designed and implemented by those that will use the technology have the best chance of succeeding. However, the existence of a technocracy makes it less likely that the users will have control of or even a significant role in designing or implementing a new system.

As part of the bureaucratic apparatus, the technocracy has learned to play the game of defending turf and is no longer able to provide leadership or support innovation. Its turf is the installed system over which it presides. It has become the perfect manifestation of "When your only tool is a hammer, every problem looks like a nail." With the range of solutions now available to us, it is an unnecessary limitation to try to answer every problem with whatever we already have. In many cases, small scale solutions, capable of local development and administration, may not be considered if they fall outside of the control of the technocracy.

Another consequence of bureaucracy is job specialization. This is what justifies the existence of a technocracy and gives it a monopoly over library automation planning. However, it does not recognize that expertise has spread throughout the organization as more staff use and support computer installations. And much of that expertise is with newer technologies, giving them an edge over the experts in the systems office. Nor does the organization chart recognize how technology has changed the role of library paraprofessionals. Despite these changes, there is a continuing assumption that only one box on the chart has the knowledge and ability to decide what is best for the library.

This monopoly also ignores and frustrates a demand for greater control of the development process. Many of the decisions now being made about the future of the online catalog, have significant influence over the library's service mission for many years to come. Two issues being decided right now are the development of supercatalogs and providing remote access to local library systems. Reference librarians and other public service librarians have always been keenly interested in the development of library catalogs, even when there was little to decide. These new opportunities to decide the shape and function of the catalog reopen the debate about who controls this most basic of library tools.

It is this debate that most pointedly calls into question the role of the technocracy. When it comes down to it, who is more able to articulate service needs? Who is better able to act as an advocate for library users? Who best understands the catalog's role as a research tool? This expertise demands role in the planning and design for the online catalog. Instead reference librarians' role in planning for the online catalog is largely second-hand, This is unacceptable. We need to look for alternative organizational models to put control of automation planning back in the hands of those that use it.

If automation is reinventing librarianship, then we need to reinvent the library. The essential question is "How can we best use our resources?" The basic answer is that we need to redesign the organization to decentralize planning and to give more decision making power to those most directly involved. Eliminate the systems office as we know it and put the responsibility for automation planning back in the hands of individual departments. Require technical expertise in all new professional hires and create an expectation for automation planning among the librarians on staff. Find a means to reward the contributions of paraprofessionals. Let us say farewell to technocracy and hello to the future.

HYPERREF: AN EXPERT SYSTEM FOR THE REFERENCE DESK

Corinne Jörgensen and Peter Jörgensen,
Interactive Publishing

ABSTRACT

HyperRef™ solves the common problem patrons have finding appropriate reference materials when a reference librarian is not available. HyperRef is an easily customized "expert system" which guides patrons to reference items that are relevant to their information needs and requirements. Through carefully designed question negotiation screens the topic of interest, level of detail, as format and other factors are taken into account. Multiple pathways to every source ensure maximum utility by the widest possible audience. Developed jointly by a reference librarian and a software designer, HyperRef handles eighty percent of the questions asked the reference desk staff at a small liberal arts college. The system helps patrons find such diverse things as the pencil sharpener, the address of a government agency or an index to articles on a specific subject. An extensive study of reference desk activity, and a thorough knowledge of reference materials went into achieving this goal. HyperRef has an easy-to-approach user interface, designed according to well established human factors principles. Over six hundred reference items are online, as are interactive maps, and other sources of information, all readily accessed by untrained users. HyperRef can be modified to serve special collections and information centers, and can interface with other online bibliographic sources such as an online public access catalog.

1. EXPERT SYSTEMS IN REFERENCE WORK

There is a growing interest in the professional literature in the use of expert systems in reference work (Ref. 1). An expert system is a computerized system which draws upon the knowledge of experts in a field as a foundation for its database. This database can then be queried and can formulate answers according to a set of "if, then" rules.

One of the major problems in developing an expert system for reference work is the amount of time required to develop the knowledge base, as well as tailoring the system to the unique requirements of individual libraries. Additional concerns are the extent to which an expert system can adequately replace the reference interview and address the variety of questions encountered at the reference desk. This article discusses how one expert system, HyperRef, meets these concerns.

2. THE GOALS OF AN EXPERT SYSTEM

Before development of any system begins, the goals of the system must be clearly articulated. The main goals for an expert system in reference work are to provide patrons with access to materials when a reference librarian is not available and to assist the reference librarian during times of peak demand. An expert system provides answers to questions during late night or week-end hours when no reference librarian is present. The reality today is that in many libraries paraprofessionals or student assistants are staffing the reference desk during off-hours, producing concerns about the quality of assistance provided to patrons. An expert system can provide consistency in answers provided patrons by non-professional staff.

An expert system also serves as a back-up in times of peak demand. It is in the interest of good public relations to provide patrons with efficient service; an expert system can provide answers to many questions when the lines at the reference desk become too long. In addition, an expert system can serve as a back-up to the librarian for sources not often used, or in an unfamiliar subject area. This dual usage of an expert system by both patrons and librarians necessitates a flexible user interface which can lead a novice step-by-step through a search and provide an "expert" mode for more knowledgeable users.

With these goals in mind, the question then becomes whether an expert system can in fact handle a satisfactory percentage of the questions encountered at the reference desk. There are two considerations in answering this question. Can a system be developed which can successfully replace the process of question negotiation, and can a database be developed which has both the breadth and depth to address the most frequently-asked questions? There has been a huge amount written on the process of Reference question negotiation; most of this literature would suggest that the human intermediary is absolutely necessary, as library users cannot articulate their information needs, much less find what they need (Ref. 2).

There are, however, a few articles which suggest that many of the reference desk interactions which take place are routine and could be handled by an expert system: questions which fall into such categories as direction and information, simple facts, addresses and phone numbers, current events, or basic biographical information (Ref. 3). These are also the types of questions which can contribute to librarian frustration and burn-out and prevent effective handling of more complex questions because of time constraints and job pressure. Therefore these questions are ideal candidates for a reference desk expert system.

An expert system for reference is thus not intended to duplicate the functions of the reference librarian, nor to duplicate the function of the card or online catalog. The system serves as a screening device for both librarian and patron alike. As library collections expand and library services become computerized, there is more and more need for effective filtering devices to serve as gateways to the vast amounts of information contained in a library.

2.1. Development

In order to evaluate whether an expert system could in fact handle a satisfactory percentage of the reference questions encountered at a small liberal arts college reference desk, a two-semester survey of reference desk questions was conducted by one librarian. During the two semesters over 1600 reference questions were logged and the sources for answers were recorded. The questions were then analyzed and grouped into categories by broad subject area and by topic (a subject area is a traditional area such as "art" while a topic is more informal, and includes such areas as "company information").

The questions were categorized by level, such as "beginning research" or "in need of advanced or specialized material." They were also categorized by whether a reference librarian's intervention was seen as necessary. Therefore, a question may have been easily answerable by a common source, but if the manner in which the question was asked would have necessitated question negotiation by a librarian, it was categorized as needing a reference librarian's intervention. Questions for which ready-reference online searching was necessary, such as citation verification and tracking, also fall into this latter category.

The results of the survey indicated that from 60% to 80% of the questions encountered at the reference desk could be categorized into a few major categories and handled by major sources. The percentage dropped somewhat during the course of the second semester because of a new senior thesis requirement, which required more assistance in advanced research and online searching.

In addition, other reference librarians were surveyed about the nature of their reference desk interactions, and asked for input on their most often-used sources for answers. This information correlated highly with the results of the reference question survey.

These results formed the basis for the development of the knowledge base for the HyperRef system. By concentrating on the needs of the users, it represents somewhat of a departure from the more usual methodology of developing an expert system, which relies more heavily on the knowledge of the expert (Ref. 4). The interface design provides a more flexible approach to information than the heavily subject-oriented methods used in library classification schemes by incorporating as an organizing principle information on how patrons themselves characterize their information needs.

2.2. Design Considerations

The system design drew heavily on information gathered in the survey to provide understandable and meaningful access points to reference sources. The iterative design process, (the cyclical process of testing a system and using the input to modify the it), was very important in further refining access points and the user interface. Iterative design helped pinpoint problem areas, such as overuse of library "jargon," and improved overall system design and performance.

The system assumes a basic ability among users to categorize an information need in broad terms. Research suggests that users will approach a computerized information system in a different manner than they will approach a human information source (Ref. 5). HyperRef has been designed so that there are multiple paths to each source, recognizing that patrons will vary in their approaches to both categorizing and finding a piece of information. The system provides a flexible approach to accommodate these individual differences and thereby prevents frustration.

As mentioned above, HyperRef is not designed to duplicate the card or online catalog. It does not include every book in the reference collection or in standard reference bibliographies, but rather only those used most often by reference librarians to answer questions (the current database consists of about 650 titles). It is also designed to provide access to individual titles which may be difficult to search in the card or online catalog.

Because the system is completely open to modification, the database is easily changed to reflect an individual library's collection or usage patterns. Buttons or records can be added to accommodate special projects or special needs of specific courses. The system can be modified to provide access to a branch library, such as a science library, or to special collections, which are often uncataloged or may have unique cataloging.

The system includes visual sources of information such as maps and visual keys such as icons. The interface graphics are, however, kept very simple, with images used to reinforce or convey additional information. The graphic capabilities of newer computers tend to be overused and can foster interfaces which end up confusing the user with a cluttered screen.

3. DESCRIPTION OF SYSTEM

HyperRef is a HyperCard™ stack which, in addition to providing answers to reference questions, can function as an "expert system shell." The open design of the system allows it to be completely modifiable to accommodate individual libraries' differences. The basic program consists of several components: Help, location information (including maps), question negotiation, and book records.

The help section is designed to help the patron who is unfamiliar with the Macintosh computer. It explains the basic navigational technique of HyperRef, i.e. using the mouse to click on-screen buttons and list items, as well as how to scroll through a list that is too large for one display. As with the entire program, the help section can be customized to best address the needs of the users of a particular library.

Location information is accessed from a "Where is..." screen, a portion of which is reproduced in figure 1.

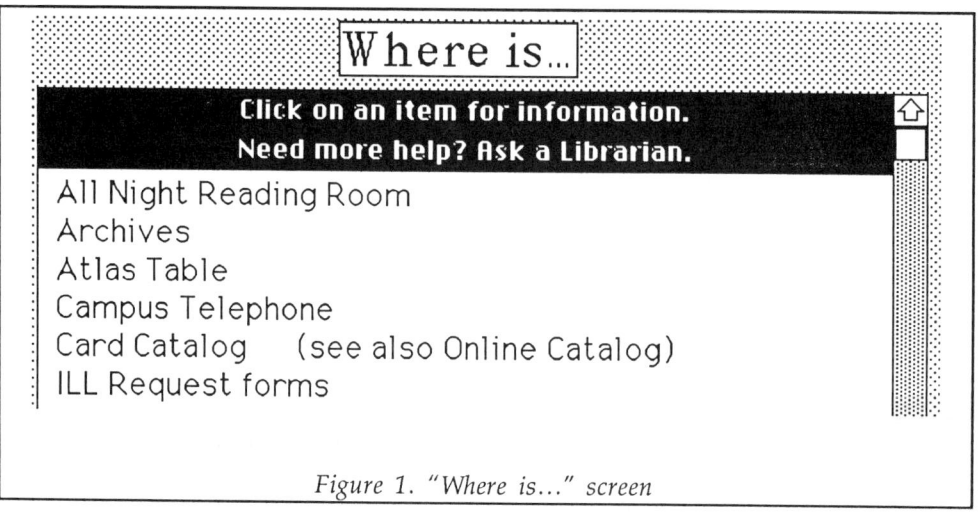

Figure 1. "Where is..." screen

Clicking on any of these items will display a map of the library with the item's location clearly highlighted (figure 2) and some explanatory text in a popup box.

Question negotiation is accomplished through a series of screens that present choices to the patron. The choices that the patron makes establish the context of the information need, including the level of need (basic or advanced), the format (journal or book) and domain. The first choice is the subject area/topic. The user clicks on the button representing the topic of interest, *e.g.* "Colleges" (see Figure 3). The topics included in the system represent those most frequently requested by the patrons of a college library. Simply pointing to any button with the mouse will display a brief explanation of that topic's scope in the central box.

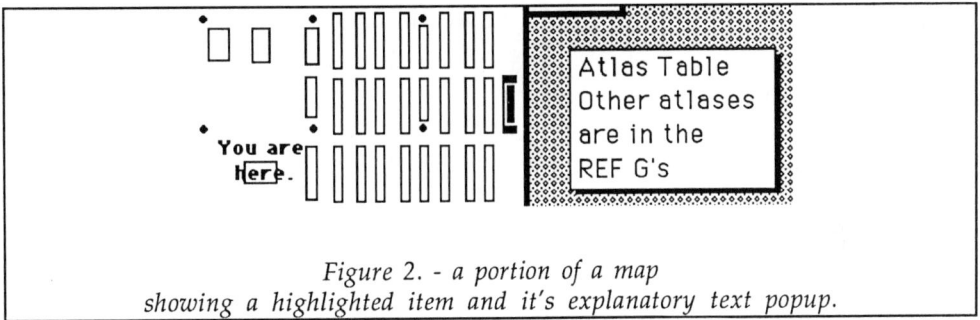

Figure 2. - a portion of a map showing a highlighted item and it's explanatory text popup.

If the user needs information in a specific subject area such as "Architecture" then she would choose the "A Specific Topic" button. This would initiate a sequence of several additional screens to determine her level of need and exact topic. Of course the ultimate goal is to help the user find one or more books or indexes. This information is presented in lists.

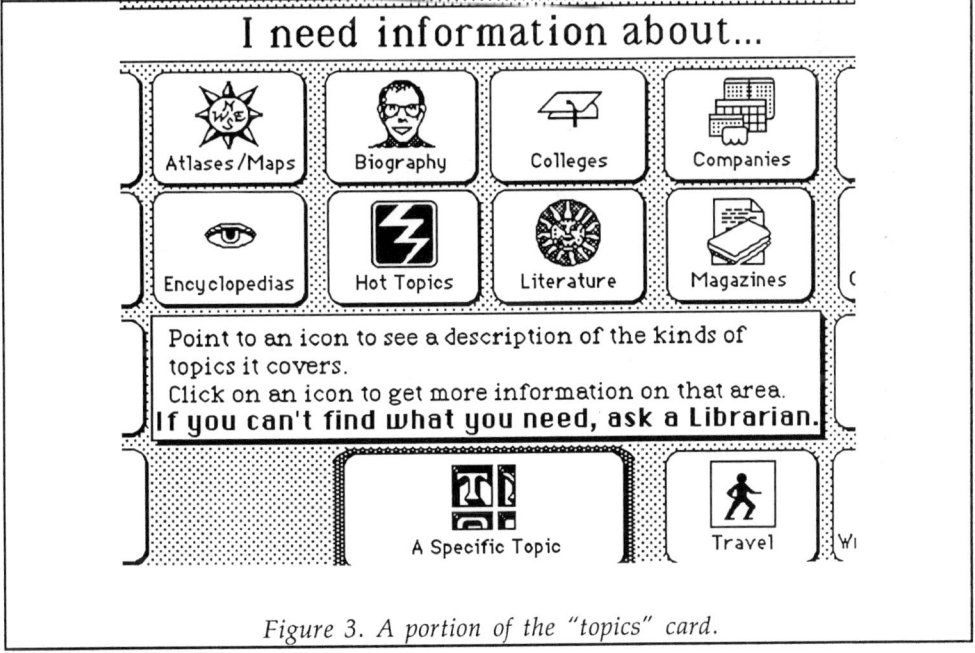

Figure 3. A portion of the "topics" card.

Clicking on one of the items displays its complete record (Figure 4) from which its location on a map can be displayed (by clicking a "Map" button).

All screens have buttons to allow backtracking ("Go Back") and quitting ("Done").

Call Number	REF L 901 .B32 1986
Title	Barron's Profiles of American Colleges
Author	Compiled and edited by the College Division of Barron's Educational Series
Edition	15th ed.
City	Woodbury, NY
Publisher	Barron's Educational Series
Date	1986
Misc.	
Description	

Figure 4. A book record.

4. ADVANTAGES OF COMPUTER

The advantages of a computer based system for reference patron assistance are numerous (Ref. 6). The major advantages are extended availability of reference service, consolidation of expertise and standardization of service.

Few if any libraries can afford to staff a reference desk around the clock with professional reference librarians, however the computer can be available twenty-four hours a day. This has obvious implications for larger libraries that have extended hours. When the reference desk is unattended an expert system can provide a base level of access support that often will satisfy the patron's information need. At times when the reference desk is staffed by non-professional personnel an expert system can help them provide quick and accurate help also.

The expertise of the entire reference staff can be consolidated into one source. This allows subject-specialist reference librarians to effectively deal with questions outside their area, again improving the overall efficiency and effectiveness of the reference department.

In an academic library a group of students (in a class) may come to the reference desk at different times with the same question (based on a particular assignment). In these cases it may be important to insure that each student gets the same help. A computerized system that is customizable, such as HyperRef, can be programmed to provide a bibliography or suggest a list of sources chosen in advance for this particular assignment by the area specialist. This not only insures that all students will receive the same level of help, but will also prevent reference desk staff from having to repeatedly generate an answer to the same question.

5. AN EXPANDED ROLE FOR EXPERT SYSTEMS IN REFERENCE

It is well-known that the implementation of a computerized system often carries with it unexpected consequences. The implementation of an expert system for reference is no different. However, with careful consideration of system capabilities and organizational factors, an expert system can function as more than just a mechanism for generating answers to reference questions.

One advantageous aspect of a computerized expert system is the possibility of reaching users that reference librarians are otherwise unable to reach. As reference librarians know, some people are loath to ask questions of a person, yet may be willing to try out a computerized system on their own. Computer phobia, a possible drawback, is also becoming less and less of an issue for the student population as more and more students are being exposed to computers in high school and are using them for word-processing in their courses.

Another unanticipated function of an expert system is that it can accomplish some of the goals of traditional bibliographic instruction. During use of such a system a certain amount of learning about the library and its organization takes place. HyperRef was not designed to provide bibliographic instruction, but with carefully considered additions to the program much more learning could be supported. One such promising area is in the provision of instruction for searching a library's online catalog.

In addition, with the move to PC-based systems, it becomes possible for libraries (within proper site-licensing considerations of the system in use) to "give the library" to students. A program such as HyperRef runs on a PC (the Macintosh), fits on one floppy diskette, contains a database of important reference sources, and guides the student in the appropriate use of these sources. A student could generate an initial research bibliography before even coming to the library to access basic sources. Librarians' time is thus freed up to deal with more advanced, complex questions.

An easily modifiable system can also be used to take care of individual libraries' problem areas. For instance, in many libraries signage is a problem, and there are often both physical and political reasons underlying this situation. HyperRef can be used to address existing problems such as this that have no other easily implementable solutions.

6. INTERFACING WITH OTHER LIBRARY SYSTEMS

As mentioned above, an expert system can support library goals other than providing access to reference materials. It can also be directly interfaced with other library systems, providing both a "friendlier" user interface and a more efficient means of searching the library's collections.

6.1. As a Front End

An expert system can be the basis of a front-end for an online catalog. Through its question negotiation steps it provides the patron with a clearer idea of her information need and the subject area(s) involved. This leads to two likely extensions of such systems. First, the patron could be presented with a list of likely subject headings which she would then search in the online catalog from the same computer. Alternatively, such a search could be initiated automatically, and the results displayed in real time. A variation of these scenarios would first present the material contained in the database, and then allow the patron to expand that list through an automatic online search. Browsing the circulating collection in relevant call number areas is another approach.

6.2. To Gather Statistics

Many libraries are interested in gathering usage statistics, either to assist in collection development decisions, or for staffing and budgetary considerations. An expert system can be designed to automatically gather this data for periodic review and analysis. This would be especially useful during hours when the reference desk is not staffed and manual tallying is therefore not possible.

6.3. To provide a feedback channel

In an unattended setting a stand-alone assistance system can provide a means for patron feedback. Patrons could leave messages to the staff if the results of a particular interaction were unsatisfactory, or certain books were found to be missing, etc. The anonymous nature of these "notes" and the immediate availability of the medium would tend to promote communication from patron to staff.

7. **FUTURE DIRECTIONS**

The continued evolution of desktop computers into ever-more powerful systems is driving computing towards the model of distributed rather than centralized processing. In such a model, powerful desktop computers are networked together with larger database servers. Much of the processing is done "locally" on the desktop machines while the servers handle requests for database searches. Applications such as HyperRef readily fit into this model as both stand-alone point-of-need information sources and as intelligent front-ends for database servers.

---

1. For a more detailed discussion of expert systems and a summary of recent systems being developed for reference work, see Donald E.Riggs, "Productivity Increases in Public Services: Are Expert Systems the Answer?" *Journal of Library Administration* 9 (4): 89-99, 1988.
2. See O. Gene Norman, "The Reference Interview: An Annotated Bibliography," *Reference Services Review* 7 (1): 71-77, Jan./Mar. 1979.
3. Robert Hauptman, "The Myth of the Reference Interview." *Reference Librarian* 16: 47-52, Winter 1986.
4. For a description of this process see John Richardson Jr., "Toward and Expert System for Reference Service: A Research Agenda for the 1990's." *College & Research Libraries* 50(2): 231-248, March 1989.
5. Beth Ann Hockey and Brian Nielsen, "Linguistic Analysis of Reference Transactions: If You Want an Answer, You've Got to Find a Question." *Library Software Review* 7:193, May/June 1988.
6. John Richardson Jr., "Toward and Expert System for Reference Service..." p.246-48.

CHOICES: COLLECTION MANAGEMENT ISSUES OF THE IOLS

George S. Machovec and Dennis R. Brunning, Arizona State University and Joyce Plaza, Pharmaceutical Information Service

Abstract: Libraries are moving into the electronic environment and acquiring a growing number of products in electronic formats. With the advent of CD-ROMs, locally loaded databases on institutional OPACs or mainframes, gateways to remote online systems and other electronic products libraries are having to cope with a whole new array of collection management choices. What electronic databases should be acquired, should print products be dropped in favor of electronic access, and how should selection and deselection decisions be made. Libraries will require rethinking of how librarians approach collection management of vital resources which take into account new technology, new opportunities and changing organizational structures.

1. INTRODUCTION

Increasingly, integrated online library systems (IOLS) are offering multiple databases including indexing/abstracting services, full-text, directories, local informational tools and other sources. The development of "supercatalogs," once the activity of only a few large research libraries, is now taking place at a variety of institutions (Ref. 1). Libraries are also beginning to do database resource sharing through the local loading of files and then networking (typically via leased lines or through the Internet) these products with other libraries. This means that only one institution will have to pay for the disk space and networked access from other sites is only limited by the remote site paying the licensing fee.

This evolution of the supercatalog comes hard on the heels of recent developments in CD-ROM databases. The installed based of CD-ROM products in university and research libraries is extensive and growth for this technology appears promising. In addition, CD-ROM products are now increasingly being distributed by libraries on a broader scale through in-house local area networks (LANS) which in some cases may be connected to the IOLS, or other campus, regional, or national communication networks

These developments create mixed information environments which allow the distribution of electronic products in an almost unlimited fashion.

The collection management issues of these developments are staggering. Little has been discussed in the literature on the issues or the problems of selecting, deselecting or financing electronic products. In the best of possible worlds (a deep pocket, computer literate staff) selecting and deselecting would be done as staff attempt to offer the best services at the lowest cost to the patron. In the real world a considerable challenge exists because of inflation, limited finances and the momentum of traditional thinking. How a library decides what databases to purchase (selection), whether to cancel print products when electronic equivalents are available, in what format should material be acquired, the delivery mechanism, and organizational changes present a considerable challenge.

2.   ELECTRONIC DATABASE SELECTION

The selection of electronic databases in a library environment whether they be CD-ROMs, locally loaded files, or networked access to electronic products is a major budgetary consideration. The criteria for selecting these products or services will widely vary depending on institutional priorities.

2.1 Criteria for Database Selection

At Arizona State University a set of criteria were developed to assist in database selection for locally loading files in the IOLS (at ASU it is the CARL system). Many of these same issues are valid for other electronic products such as CD-ROMs (Ref. 3).

> Cost. The cost of purchasing or leasing an electronic service is foundational in the decision process. For locally loaded files, it is important to acquire products with no connect hour or hit charges otherwise the cost is uncontrolled. The cost of backfiles must also be considered in addition to current annual subscription rates.
>
> Disk storage. For locally loaded databases the hard disk storage to load a file can sometimes be considerable. In some cases the lease/purchase price is minor when compared with this issue. Large files such as Medline and Chemical Abstracts are often not good candidates for local loading for this reason. In these instances, dial-in or gatewaying may be a more cost effective solution.
>
> Backfile availability. Are backfiles available and for how many years? It may not be worth it to get an electronic product if retrospective data are important and enough is not yet available in machine readable form.
>
> Size of clientele served. Since most organizations have a limited number of databases to locally acquire, those which reach the broadest base of users may be of priority.
>
> Preeminence of program supported. The importance and prestige of certain departments or users may influence which files are acquired first.
>
> Mapping the database into the local system. For locally loaded files, the ease of programming to load it into the local system may influence which files to acquire.

Searchability in local systems. What sophistication in search software is needed to successfully query the database in question? This may influence whether to acquire a file in CD-ROM, local loading or networked access.

Currency. How often is a file updated in machine readable form. If it has greater currency than the print counterpart this will influence choices.

Multidisciplinary coverage. If broad coverage for databases is desired, it may make sense to acquire databases that meet many needs.

Overlap with other electronic products. It does not normally make sense to acquire a file in more than one electronic format due to cost considerations. Is this product already available somewhere else in the institution.

Equality. Although one cannot meet everyone's needs, especially in academia, it does make sense to distribute the acquisition of databases across different disciplines to maintain some level of equity.

Inexpensive database availability through commercial search services. Some databases are available at low connect hour fees from commercial hosts (e.g. Medline). This may influence a decision on whether to lease tapes or acquire a CD-ROM, depending on the level of use and the size of the file.

3. RETENTION OF PRINT IN LIGHT OF ELECTRONIC MEDIA

Should a library retain subscriptions to printed versions of directories, handbooks, encyclopedias, indexing and abstracting services and other sources when they become available online? There is not a single simple answer to this issue and a library's decision to retain a publication in a variety of formats will depend on a number of variables.

3.1 CD-ROM and Online Catalog Databases

Databases on CD-ROM or locally loaded in online catalogs (or in other organizational mainframes), or databases available on a gateway basis have some significant differences from databases available through commercial search services. In most cases these products are acquired for some fixed fee which is absorbed by the library. In this instance the cost for searching these products is usually not born by the patron but by the library. The dilemma is that if this electronic information was also being acquired by the library in print should this print format be eliminated. In other cases a new electronic product may or may not have a direct print equivalent but it may have the same (or more) information as some other print product owned by the library.

3.2 Criteria for Decision Making

Listed are some issues that a library may want to consider when deciding whether a print product should be retained because a library now has access to an electronic equivalent (Ref. 2).

<u>Lease or purchase</u>. Is the database being acquired on a lease or purchase arrangement? Many electronic products are leased which means that if the subscription is dropped that the product has to returned to the producer or the database removed from service. In locally loaded files this means that the database can no longer be kept online and the entire database has to be removed. For CD-ROMs this may mean returning the product to the producer. If a source is considered fundamental to a library's services this would then leave a gap if the print product had been dropped.

<u>Ease of availability of print backfile</u>. How easy will it be for a library to acquire a backfile of a printed source if it is dropped and then later needs to be acquired? For example, some indexing and abstracting services are easily available from the publisher at a later date (or on the used market) while others are not.

<u>Economics</u>. If money were no problem many libraries would probably retain titles in both a print and electronic format. However, economics is a key factor in whether both can be retained. Some publishers give significant discounts for access to their databases (whether it be through a commercial timesharing service, CD-ROM or tape leasing) if the print subscription is maintained. Depending on the cost differential it may be worth keeping the print.

<u>Level of use</u>. How much use will be given to an electronic product in the library? If a CD-ROM product is being considered will it be on a stand-alone workstation or will it be networked? Locally loaded databases, such as on CARL, BRS/Search or a NOTIS platform, will support multiple users but are enough terminals available for the public? If very heavy use of an electronic product is anticipated, the need for the retention of the paper subscription may be increased or else the library will need to increase the number of workstations for access to the electronic version.

<u>Space</u>. Lack of shelf space may be one of the important motivating factors in dropping a print subscription in lieu of an electronic product. This is particularly true in special libraries where space is often at a premium.

<u>Completeness of records</u>. Is either the print or electronic product more complete than the other? As a rule of thumb, electronic databases for indexing/abstracting services are usually more complete than their printed counterparts due to cost or space limitations in paper publishing efforts. For example, many indexing services may provide subject access to only the major subject headings in a citation for the print version, while providing major and minor headings for access in the electronic environment (as well as other parts of the record). However, paper sources are usually

more complete than full text electronic sources for encyclopedias, journals or monographs as they are only beginning to include graphics and even when they do it may only be done on a limited basis because of the vast storage requirements for high resolution graphics. In addition, when graphics are included in an electronic product is the resolution adequate?

Difficulty of electronic retrieval. One of the key dilemmas facing libraries is that with the proliferation of electronic products there are many different search engines and user interfaces. This means that if a patron must search multiple products from different vendors (especially true in the CD-ROM arena) then a variety of search packages may need to be used. Although there has been much discussion about the NISO common command language as a tool to solve this dilemma, very few search engines actually have this standard available. One of the advantages of locally loaded databases in a libraries' online catalog is that all of the databases are accessible with the same search engine. However, even libraries that locally load files often also have CD-ROMs and timesharing search services.

Difficulty of the print product. Another related issue which libraries have considered in dropping a print subscription is the difficulty of use for the print product. Some printed indexes (e.g. Government Reports Announcements/Index, MLA Bibliography, Bibliography of Agriculture, Engineering Index, Biological Abstracts, Dissertation Abstracts) are notoriously time consuming or difficult to use in paper and they are easier to use in the electronic environment. If the paper product is not being used why keep it going?

Core product? Is a particular printed product considered a core publication to your clients. Although an electronic version may improve access, the presence of the printed product may be crucial for public relations, browsing and access when the electronic product is not available or in use.

Hours of availability. Will the electronic database be available during all library hours. Some libraries offer CD-ROMs or timesharing searching only during limited library hours and thus a print version must be available if it is considered a core or crucial product. However, locally loaded databases are often available for more hours than the print because the database may be accessible via dial-in or through other networking arrangements on a 24-hour per day basis.

Backfile availability. Many electronic databases (especially indexing/abstracting services) have only a limited number of years available in machine readable form. Thus to do a complete search, one will at some point, have to return to the printed sources. This may influence a decision on whether to cancel the print and will certainly influence the decision to retain print for older backfiles.

Printing and downloading. Many electronic products allow the printing or downloading of records. However, will a library provide printers and other appropriate mechanisms to enhance a patrons use of an electronic product? If a library does not provide printing or downloading capabilities, it is actually easier to capture information from the print product where photocopying may be done.

<u>Prestige of volume counts</u>. Although this may seem very anachronistic, many libraries (especially in academia) still measure their greatness on volume counts. This has provided an inertia for the retention of printed volumes even when other reasons would indicate otherwise.

<u>Library instruction</u>. Depending on the diversity and quantity of electronic products provided there may be an increased need for reference and instructional services. This may influence not cancelling printed products if a library cannot provide the needed public service support to assist patrons in the electronic media. Once again, this can work in the other direction, with the online source being easier to use and thus an incentive to cancel the print.

4. <u>DESELECTION AND RESELECTION OF ELECTRONIC DATABASES</u>

Electronic databases evolve. To remain competitive, vendors incorporate the latest technological advances. Hard on these advances come new marketing strategies--from new licensing structures to new product configurations. A new technology and the way that it is implemented and consumed remains new for only a brief period of time.

Collection managers face a set of concerns in regard to electronic databases. As collection resource tools, electronic databases are expensive. Often, they duplicate coverage of traditional sources. They are also variously and complexly priced. Technological and financial limitations create restricted resources, for example, limiting access to specific users (an information equity issue) or overall access (eg. cueing for terminals). Technology changes, creating new products and markets, which makes it hard to plan for budgets and services while creating greater user demands and expectations.

In many ways, the management of periodical indices was and remains relatively simple. Tradition almost demands that the major indexes be purchased and maintained. Certain indexing and abstracting services like Chemical Abstracts and Psychological Abstracts have always been expensive; others, like ERIC or Reader's Guide to Periodical Literature are less expensive. In any event these services are on the whole more expensive than individual journal subscriptions or monographs. However, academic libraries are expected to have these services and the cost versus use ratio is well-anticipated.

It should be evident that managing electronic collections defies this simplicity. The perennial concern of collection managers--to buy or not to buy--becomes to but to buy or not to buy, to continue to buy or lease or rent and--to break the lease.

Just as collection managers must carefully examine and resolve selection issues, they must also deal with deselection and reselection of electronic databases. A library must have clearly defined methods and policy underlying these methods to cancel databases or to shift gears and select alternatives to existing databases. As all services of the library are bound to be affected by deselection/reselection, a decision-making process that integrates all service units is crucial.

4.1 Deselection of Electronic Databases

Deselection is necessary for technological, service, economic, and political reasons. An electronic database licensing formula may be revised and put the database out of the price range of a library's database budget. For example, Wilson has recently changed its tape lease licensing formula from one figured on a basic fee plus terminal count to that of a higher base fee and potential user count. Or, using Wilson again as an example, an electronic database may be available on tape or in CD-ROM format. At Arizona State University we were offering the General Science Index and the Applied Science and Technology Index on CD-ROM but later opted to load the Wilson tapes for these indexes onto our PAC. We chose to cancel the CD-ROM product. Similarly, the CARL consortium, of which Arizona State University is an Associate Member, is planning to load the ERIC tapes. At present, we provide ERIC on CD-ROM and Wilson's Education Index via PAC. With an ERIC version available on CARL, we will be faced with a number of options, including keeping all three, dropping the CD-ROM version of ERIC but keeping EI, or canceling EI and the ERIC on CD-ROM and going just with ERIC via the OPAC.

4.2 Reselection of Electronic Databases

Libraries may also be faced with changing from one similar product to another or changing the means of access. For example, in the spring of 1989, University Microfilms Incorporated had just unveiled its OnDisc line of CD-ROM databases, including ABI/Inform OnDisc, Dissertations OnDisc, Newspaper Abstracts OnDisc, and PA OnDisc. UMI was providing full-feature retrieval software (Boolean and field searching) and CD-ROM versions of very important and popular online sources. More important, they were aggressively pricing their product line to compete with their nearest competitor, Information Access Corporation's InfoTrac For the price of a five-station InfoTrac subscription, UMI would offer a similar configuration of three of its OnDisc products.

ASU negotiated a good three year deal with UMI for access to CD-ROM databases deemed essential for our users. We reselected for somewhat similar databases. That was two summers ago. Now IAC has retooled, so to speak, and markets its InfoTrac databases with a software that retains its simple interface but supplements it with boolean search capabilities. In short, IAC rekindles our interest. We wait for the aggressive pricing.

We could elaborate--on and on. The point is that how we get information and the price we are going to pay remains quite fluid and promises to remain so. This is said in the context of high user demand for electronic databases and a equally high user expectation that electronic formats are and should be available. This is very different collection management situation than we had as late as the 1983 when buying for a library's collection was limited to buying books and subscribing to journals. There is more money at stake, more options, and an ever-evolving set of options.

5. <u>INTEGRATING DECISION MAKING IN DESELECTING/RESELECTING ELECTRONIC DATABASES</u>

Getting rid of electronic databases or changing products is a crucial move. It must be made with a good sense of the key variables at work as well as the impact on library services. Perhaps at any time in the life of a library the deselecting of a traditional resource would have been a delicate maneuver. However, in the context of an automated library, the act is both delicate and far ranging in its impact.

To begin, electronic databases are very popular and immensely successful. In terms of popularity, they are a growth industry. In a recent in-house survey conducted at ASU, patron demand could be best characterized as not "either/or" but "both/and". Patrons prefer searching for information via computer, printing results via computer, and accessing library databases from wherever a PC can be connected to the computing network. This popularity originates not in the fiscal concern of librarians for database costs but in the power of computing to find information. Chances are good that if one removes an electronic database--from a workstation, a PAC, or a network--users will notice.

Changing electronic formats also requires that a library or university have the appropriate technology and be organized to handle the new technology. For example, subscribing to a full-text database requires that the library have a way to print the information and to maintain a heavily used printing operation.

A library must also have a cost-effective, timely, and graceful way in and out of licensing contracts. Ideally, one should not negotiate a contract that locks one into a product for too long a period--but long enough to protect a good price. One should be able to review licensing fees frequently enough to deal with vendor changes. But if this isn't the case, a library should be prepared to cancel or switch databases in a fiscally sensible way. This may call for more flexible accounting practices that would allow a library to take advantage of vendor discounts and to avoid the "locking in" mechanism of encumbrances.

Most important, deselection/reselection decisions should be based on sound information about local electronic database use and how that use will be affected by changing products or means of access, canceling the product, or otherwise shifting user options. Collection managers should survey user demands and expectations not only in a reactive sense of looking at terminal counts but proactively. We need to ask our patrons, what if we did this but not that--how would this affect your use of our resources?

Public service units also need to be brought into the decision making process. The use of electronic databases has significantly impacted reference, document delivery, and instructional services. These services have traditionally worked with accessing information, collection management, with stocking the documents. Now collection management is very much involved with access. Collection management decisions will affect what tools reference librarians work with, what items will be demanded through ILL, and what tools will need to be taught.

More than ever before decision making needs to be integrated. Collection managers are in a good position to coordinate the decision making. This is not a new role. In the traditional model, bibliographers have selected materials under the direction of collection managers who established collection development guidelines. Presumably these guidelines were established by knowledge of what users required. Collecting electronic databases works within a similar model but now it is the librarians concerned with access to information who must be consulted. And we may not be collecting databases in a permanent sense as the word implies. Rather, we are assembling products and services that are the best deal for patrons and the library at a given point in time.

Collection managers, however, need to recognize a new paradigm in libraries. Technology has shifted primary emphasis away from printed documents to information resources. The library is no longer simply a collection whose major finding tools are themselves collectibles. Instead the library is a set of constantly evolving resources. The common denominator is the computer as a information retrieval and communication tool.

Actually the task of collection managers is library resources husbandry, the good, careful, management of resources. Never a phrase that will grace the title of a Collection Manager but to the point. The library as a place where documents are stored and used if and only if you find them is a view from the past.

6. REFERENCES

1. Potter, William Gray. Expanding the Online Catalog. Information Technology and Libraries 8, No. 2, p. 99-104, June 1989.

2. Machovec, George S. The Retention of Print Sources in View of Electronic Databases 16, No. 3, pp. 26-28, September 1990.

3. Machovec, George S. Locally Loaded Databases in Arizona State University's Online Catalog Using the CARL System. Information Technology and Libraries 8, No. 2, p. 161-171, June 1989.

SELECTION AND ADAPTATION OF LIBRARY SYSTEMS IN A CHANGING ENVIRONMENT

Sharon B. Mehl, Scitex Corporation Ltd.

Keywords: Integrated Online Library Systems, Technical Processes and Services, Communication Systems, Information Retrieval.

Abstract: This paper discusses the adaptation of online library systems in a changing environment in a high-technology company.

Four systems are discussed. These are a library management system, including an in-house database and thesaurus; a second system purchased specifically for the management and retrieval of a large patent collection; and a communication system integrating the online database hosts, and the downloading and distribution of information within the company. A very significant addition has recently been made. This is the purchase of an OPAC system based on a VAX mainframe, with multi-user possibilities. The present PC-based system will be replaced by the mainframe with multiple access, and the data converted to the new system.

The emphasis in this paper is placed on the co-operation between the library staff and the Management Information System (MIS) department of the company. Library holdings and online information must be made available throughout the company, as well as to overseas subsidiaries. This is being done by means of mainframe VAX and HP computer networks, as well as via PC-based networks. The construction and operation of the network are discussed.

Finally, adaptability and vendor support are considered. All of the library management systems are manufactured locally. Thus, we have been able to change and technically adapt the systems to our needs. The exciting and interesting aspects of these processes are highlighted, as we work side-by-side with computer staff in achieving our goals.

1.   INTRODUCTION

This paper considers the selection and adaption of integrated online library systems and a communications system on a network, to a changing environment in a high-technology company. Scitex Corporation Ltd. designs, manufactures, markets and services interactive computer color imaging systems used primarily in the printing and publishing industries. Scitex operates marketing, sales and service divisions in North America, Europe and Japan.

The various systems discussed here have evolved over a period of eight years. The library management systems are all manufactured in Israel. The online communications system and the network on IBM Personal Computers have been developed by Scitex itself, through the MIS (Management Information Systems) department. This has enabled us to engineer various changes in the systems, and adapt them to our needs. What I hope to make clear in this paper is the growth that the Company has experienced from a PC-based system, used only by the library staff, to an OPAC (Online Patron Access Catalog) on a mainframe computer, used by employees throughout the company, with various access points. At the same time, a very sophisticated communications systems has been developed inhouse, which has now been in operation for some years.

2.   THE SCOPE OF THE PAPER

The paper will give a brief description of the four library management systems, and the practical advantages and disadvantages of each. It will also describe the evolution and installation of the communications system and network.

3.   AUTOMATIC/TECHNICAL REQUIREMENTS OF THE INFORMATION CENTER

At the outset, there were two clear divisions in the requirements of the information center. The first was a communications network for online search and dispersal of information, and the second was a library management system. This was needed to deal with acquisitions, periodical routing and claims, and bibliographical functions such as cataloging, authority files, loans and circulation. We also needed a system that would provide the facilities for an inhouse database with keyword indexing, and an online thesaurus.

In summary, we needed a system that could tackle library management and housekeeping problems while providing effective and exact information retrieval. We also needed an effective communications system, with access to several database hosts, and the ability to distribute the information electronically.

4.   OUR FIRST LIBRARY MANAGEMENT SYSTEM

Eight years ago, when I began actively looking to automate the library, the information center was less than one year old. It was not practical at the time to consider a turnkey system or an integrated online system that ran on a mainframe. My dream at that time was an integrated system that would combine public access with library functions on the same computer (Ref.1). We began investigating PC-based library management systems.

One of our most important considerations in the selection process was that it should be manufactured locally. We felt that this was very important with regard to vendor support and logistic and operational problems. Fortunately, the system that we chose, LMS PLUS, is manufactured in Israel and answered our requirements. LMS PLUS runs on all XT and AT personal computers and PS/2 (including compatibles). It operates under MS-DOS and PC networks such as Novell. The system supports multi-user environments. It can download data to other databases, and accept data (upload) from them. It does require at least 10 Mb storage, and 256K memory.

The information center circulates a bi-weekly list of articles of interest from professional journals. It was essential that the system included a good inhouse database with a thesaurus facility. This was well supplied by Top Systems. We built our own thesaurus, based on the INSPEC Thesaurus (Ref.2), the ACM "Computing Reviews" Classification System (Ref.3), and the PIRA Keyword Listing (Ref.4). Our subject areas are computer software, pattern recognition, computer graphics, image processing, color and prepress electronic publishing technologies.

The problems that arose with the LMS system were mainly in the areas of periodical controls and claims. Many of those problems have been ameliorated through an active users group, which meets regularly with the vendors of the system. Scitex has worked with LMS for eight years. Owing to the growth in research and development, however, and the subsequent increase in professional staff, it was increasingly clear that patrons had to have access to the library's holdings. The company is also spread throughout several buildings, and there are subsidiaries abroad, so a network system was needed.

The company operates two networks based on HP and VAX systems, and company policy was not prepared to support another network. Therefore, a library management system had to be chosen that operated on one of the existing systems. Thus we arrived at the decision to purchase ALEPH.

6.   ALEPH (AUTOMATED LIBRARY EXPENDABLE PROGRAM HEBREW UNIVERSITY)

ALEPH is an online, real-time, integrated library management system developed at the Hebrew University of Jerusalem (Ref.5). It provides a full range of library services. The advantage of

Aleph is that it is modular, so that one can use only those components which are relevant to one's needs. It is a table-driven system. Aleph supports networks of libraries in different sites.

ALEPH was particularly attractive to us because it allows browsing through catalogs, Boolean commands for searching, and the ability to limit or expand the search. The types of access that it allows to the database are authorities, (e.g., titles, subjects, authors); indexes; and words (from titles, abstracts, etc.) As in LMS, it enables display of the items' abstract. It also offers authority file and thesaurus maintenance, retrieval, circulation, acquisition and inter-library loan management.

We have only recently purchased Aleph, and are in the process of installing it, and converting the holdings from LMS to Aleph. We look forward to the multi-user possibilities on the VAX, which is a Scitex supported computer system. We are positive about the different approach from patrons that the multi-user aspect will bring about.

7. SAPIR

Sapir is a library management system that has been developed locally and which runs on the IBM Personal Computer. It is flexible and user-friendly, and its periodical control facilities are very good. The prime reason that we bought a second PC-based system was that we needed a separate system for our expanding patent collection. The patent collection could not be available on a multi-user system, due to the need for confidentiality.

I enclose examples of screens, and elaborate on excellent user-friendly features.

8. ELECTRONIC COMMUNICATIONS SYSTEM AND NETWORK

A full description is given of the Scitex Communication Network, Scinet, which provides automatic connection to the following database hosts: Dialog, Data-Star, Orbit Search Services, Maxwell Online, Reuters, Profile Information, and Dun and Bradstreet's Dunsprint. This has been in operation for some years. The electronic network on the IBM Personal Computer enables the downloaded information to be sent directly to the client by means of electronic mail. Examples and case histories will be given.

9. ADAPTABILITY, VENDOR & USER - SUPPORT

All the systems that we use allow for changes. We have, indeed, made additions and adapted our own requirements. Examples are given. We are, and have been, greatly assisted by our MIS (Management Information Systems) staff, with regard to PC's.

With the new system, Aleph, we are being assisted by the VAX installation staff. A three-way cooperation has evolved between the library staff, the vendors, and the Scitex computer hardware and software problems. Certain cases are described. The support received from the vendors and the Scitex computer staff is emphasized.

10. CONCLUSION

This synopsis offers a brief outline of the evolution of and reasons for the various integrated online library systems employed by the Scitex Information Center and Library. At the same time, it attempts to show the development in electronic communication systems and networks developed by the Company itself. It also offers a personalised view of systems that are available in Israel.

REFERENCES

1. Lynch, Clifford A. Linking library automation systems in the Internet functional requirements, planning, and policy issues. Library Hi Tech. Issue 28. pp.7-18.

2. Inspec Thesaurus, 1989. The Institution of Electrical Engineers, 1989. 518 p.

3. CR Classification System. Computing Reviews. January 1990. Association for Computing Machinery. pp. 9-20.

4. Keyword listing: A search tool for the Pira database. Pira Information Services. 58 p.

5. Levi, Judith. Aleph: an online real-time integrated library system. Judaica Librarianship. 1 (2) Spring 84, pp. 58-63. illus.

LIBRARY AND COMPUTING STAFF: LEARNING FROM ONE ANOTHER

Ray E. Metz, Case Western Reserve University

Keywords: Administration of Technology, Computer Science, Librarians, Libraries, Computing Centers, Library Information Technologies

Abstract: A growing segment of influential members of higher education administrations feel that the professional staffs of libraries and computing centers should be drawn tighter together organizationally. We have begun to see specific institutions of higher education group such professionals under the same organizational structure.

Case Western Reserve University has both libraries and computing center professionals reporting to its Vice President for Information Services. Library Information Technologies as it applies to all campus libraries has been organized as a separate department with a director reporting to the Vice President as a peer of other directors of libraries and computing.

This paper addresses a variety of aspects concerning such closer working relationships. The opportunities for sharing between library and computing professionals are significant and need to be capitalized upon for the organization to benefit. This paper also presents information concerning some important factors relevant to ensuring a good working relationship between these groups.

1. INTRODUCTION

One of the most important challenges currently facing academic librarianship is a basic challenge to its role of information provider on the academic campus. That challenge, which could bring about significant changes to the profession, is coming from our computing professional colleagues. While the profession of librarianship may be facing a challenge, the actual responsibilities of the profession are certain to be continued -- even if they are given to individuals not known as librarians. It is the current generation of librarians who will determine what the next generation of librarians is called.

Librarianship at Case Western Reserve University (CWRU) is currently addressing this issue. CWRU is a private institution of higher education located in Cleveland serving approximately 8,000 students with four autonomous library structures. In 1988 the position of Vice-President for Information Services was created. The appointment included the responsibility for general computing on the campus as well as the application of technology in the libraries on campus. Computing and library staff working on technology in the libraries found themselves in a somewhat ambiguous organizational structure. In September of 1991 the University Library began reporting directly to the Vice President for Information Services. At the same time the position of Director of Library Information Technologies which also reports directly to the Vice President was created. This created a structure which has some librarians, computing professionals, and a separate group of library/computing professionals all reporting through one administrative structure. What has resulted is an opportunity to see how important it is for librarians and computing professionals to work together as colleagues.

2. LIBRARY INFORMATION TECHNOLOGIES

The creation of Library Information Technologies Department (LIT) is a reflection of the goals and objectives of Information Services. Two important reasons for the formation were:

- LIT's responsibilities go beyond the boundaries of any one library on campus and therefore should not report to one particular library and librarian
- LIT's responsibilities are strategic in importance to the goals of Information Services and therefore should report directly to the Vice President for Information Services

The current staff consists of a director, two professionals supporting a local library system, a library microcomputer lab supervisor/library network administrator, and numerous student assistants. This staff is responsible for the previous responsibilities associated with supporting traditional library automation applications as well as expanding the responsibilities of the department. That expansion is further outlined in the job description of the Director of Library Information Technologies provided.

3. DEFINITIONS OF PROFESSIONS

Library Science has been defined as "the body of organized knowledge -- in whatever form -- which is concerned with the purposes, objectives, and functions of libraries and the principles, theories, methods, organization, and techniques, employed in performing library service" (Ref. 1). Librarianship has been defined as "the application of this knowledge in the collection, organization, preservation, and use of books and other materials in libraries and in the continuous improvement and extension of library service" (Ref. 2).

Computer Science has been defined as "the body of knowledge pertaining to the automatic processing of symbolic information" (Ref. 3) and has "three broad areas of concern: the methods (algorithms) for deriving information with synthetic processors (computers) and the limitations of those methods, the physical representation of symbolic information for computation, and the design of effective processing systems" (Ref. 4).

For us to work together we need to understand each other's professions better. From the above definitions one can see that computer professionals can offer new ways for the library profession to accomplish its work. One can also see that while computing professionals need to be working with library professionals, the library seems to be only one area of concern for them out of many. Also noticeable is the focus of librarianship on the actual collection and servicing that collection and those who use it. Computer professionals by this definition lack a central concern over what the information may be, but rather focus on processing that information and also designing systems that process it.

4. COMPUTING PROFESSIONALS' EXPERIENCE WITH TRADITIONAL LIBRARY RESPONSIBILITIES

As the two groups of professionals begin to work together, it is important to look at what experience computing professionals have in some of the key areas of librarians' responsibilities.

A. Developing Collections of Information

While some computing professionals may be involved in some specific projects which may involve the acquisition of data sets, I have not found a computing center which has developed the kind of collection development sense which exists in most libraries. This sense of obligation to acquire and serve the entire university community is growing, but it is still a relatively new concept.

B. Organizing Information

Computing professionals have extensive experience with organizing information at the system architecture level; however, the actual organization of that information in presentation seems of less concern. This is a major difference between us. Librarians must work with computing professionals to ensure that they understand the importance of giving this structure to users. It is not enough to say that the information is available, it must be easily obtainable as well.

C. Preservation of Information

Computing professionals are very experienced with preserving information by doing operational backups, but the concept of long term commitment to preserving information and data seems to potentially be a trade off for newer, quicker, and bigger products and projects. The concern -- the almost instinctual concern librarians have -- for preserving information has contributed to our current problem of being perceived as potential museum keepers; however, the concept of preserving information is central to librarianship and must not be lost. What is needed is some work to ensure that our computing colleagues also begin to see the long term impacts of some of the technological projects we are undertaking for the university community.

D. Use of Information

Computing professionals on campus have often been responsible for ensuring that the machines operate and that those machines and software are available for campus users. While certainly some computing professionals in users services units have been concerned with the use of information, the primary concern has been to see that specific computer resources are available. Librarians are not only concerned that information be made available, they are also concerned that users are fully supported in using that information and supported fairly across the disciplines.

E. Continuous Improvement and Extension of Information Service

Both library and computing professionals believe strongly in the importance of their professional responsibilities. Librarians have perhaps been more concerned with service issues because of our history. Computing and library professionals are both concerned with carrying out their responsibilities in ways that will require as little intervention as possible.

5. POSITIVE AND NEGATIVE ASPECTS

The most important positive aspect of these two groups working together is the opportunity to build upon the strengths and knowledge of each group. Having computing professionals easily accessible and willing to assist in technological issues benefits the institution. The most important negative aspect is the amount of professional time involved to accomplish closer working relationships.

Some of the other positives of these two groups working together include:

- potentially stronger voice within the university structure
- validation of each unit's concerns of service and equipment needs
- librarian's better understanding of technological capabilities
- possibility of quicker integration of technologies in the library
- possibility of long term planning for computing
- increased service awareness within computing
- increased expectations for library service
- computing professionals become better informed about issues beyond "how much storage it takes to store the Library of Congress"

Some of the other negatives aspects of these two groups working together include:

- possible loss of autonomy and control
- possible loss of either profession's priorities
- possible loss of balance between planning for the future and providing for today
- discovery that our computing colleagues are paid more for similar service responsibilities (can be negative for organization if not addressed)

Librarians and computing professionals have both experienced paranoia in the concern over who is going to be in control and what negative things may happen if the "other" profession assumes responsibility. This concern needs to be handled sensitively and followed up with consistent and fair management of both groups whether or not they become part of one organizational reporting structure or not. Establishing trust and respect is imperative for such ventures to work.

6. HOW SHOULD I ORGANIZE SUCH GROUPS?

There are several ways of bringing the two group together; however, in the near future it seems unlikely that one particular organizational structure will be appropriate for colleges and universities. Each institution must decide what will work with its existing environment and personnel. Bringing the two groups of professionals organizationally together can work, but *working* together and not organizational structure is the key.

7. RECOMMENDATIONS FOR "MAKING IT WORK"

- listen to each other
- support from university, computing, library administrations
- projects and involvement at all levels of organization
- working with issues of mutual concern

- building on similarities
- "we/they" environment not tolerated
- position description/salary reviews for equity between professional groups
- substantive involvement in each other's organization
- providing ways to show each group the strengths of the other group (presentations, individual assistance)
- substantive involvement in each other's professional organizations
- organizing information services or projects so that some services are led by people from computing and others from the library

8. CONCLUSIONS

If there are so many differences then why should library and computing professionals be working together? The answer is in the learning that takes place. Librarianship needs to be challenged periodically to ensure that it is indeed doing what it is supposed to do. We can learn from computing professionals who question many of our assumptions. On the other hand, the same computing professionals have some learning to do in the area of user services and the importance of information content.

Computer science has been understandably more driven by technology and opportunity than library science has been. With current storage capabilities, network developments, decreasing needs of central mainframes with increasing numbers of work stations, and a growing need for technology-based solutions to library problems, it seems understandable that computing professionals and university administrators would begin to see the potential of building closer relationships between the two groups.

If we are to work together we need to better understand each other and our professional cultures. More important than understanding, we need to each make some changes in those cultures if we are to have a long term relationship develop. There are reasons why each of our professions has the values that they do. Blindly discarding either profession's values weakens us both. The need to work together exists now. It is up to each one of us to see that something happens.

9. SUMMARY

Some of the very foundations of librarianship are being questions by computing professionals. This questioning serves some important purposes for librarianship and is offering opportunities to work with a knowledgeable group of professionals on some of the most important issues facing the library profession. Using computing professionals as knowledgeable and respected resources on these issues benefits both groups. Each brings some unique talents, values, and knowledge to the issues. Part of Case Western Reserve University's attempts to address these issues has been to create Library Information Technologies reporting to the Vice President for Information Services along with libraries and computing.

Whether or not tomorrow's professionals carrying out the responsibilities of librarianship as we know it today are called librarians depends on the actions of today's librarians; however, librarianship and librarians will not go away just because someone else is responsible. In fact, our users and the profession itself could benefit from such a restructure. Whichever direction the future takes, it is imperative that librarians work with computing professionals for the foreseeable future -- to make sure that the important lessons and values of librarianship are included in whatever information future exists.

10. REFERENCES

1. Gates, Jean Key. Introduction to Librarianship. New York: McGraw-Hill, 1968, p. 133.

2. Ibid., p. 133.

3. The New Encyclopædia Britannica: Macropædia, 1989 ed. s.v. "Computer Science."

4. Ibid., s.v. "Computer Science."

Director of Library Information Technologies
Information Services - Case Western Reserve University

General Responsibilities:

The Director of Library Information Technologies reports to the Vice President for Information Services and is responsible for exercising dynamic leadership in the development and integration of information systems and technology as a central focus of all libraries serving the needs of Case Western Reserve University. This position is responsible for establishing all necessary working relationships, ensuring the proper budgeting of funds, implementing appropriate uses of technologies, and providing adequate training opportunities for library staff and the university community. The Director of Library Information Technologies shall also work with existing and potential consortiums concerned with access to networked information.

Specific Responsibilities:

Works with all appropriate university and non-university staff to analyze the needs of the libraries serving Case Western Reserve University concerning the use of technology in the library environment and makes recommendations on long-range planning for the use of such technology.

Develops and implements internal opportunities for training library staff in the use of new information technologies, as well as establishing formal training and intern programs with Schools of Library and Information Science.

Works closely with librarians, library staff, and other Information Services staff in setting library technology priorities.

Supervises the further development and expansion of the Case Western Reserve University local library system, including being an active participant in OHIOlink activities.

Ensures that all library technology applications are in accordance with existing or developing industry, national, and international standards and protocols.

Prepares and monitors all budgets for all areas of library technology.

Develops, implements, supports, maintains, and promotes general purpose and specialized computing including microcomputer and telecommunication support within the libraries to increase the efficiency of the human resources of the libraries serving Case Western Reserve University.

Works with appropriate faculty, staff, students, and information professionals to provide client-driven interfaces such as Cleveland Free-Net to information technology products and appropriate levels of training to use such interfaces.

Reviews and recommends to the Vice President for Information Services all technology related purchases for the libraries serving Case Western Reserve University.

Supervises the activities, the staff, and the further development of public access computer labs.

Identifies and introduces machine readable data files, locally and commercially produced, into library technology systems including network access.

Supervises the introduction and ongoing development of networked CD-ROM products including acquiring appropriate network site licenses for CD-ROM products recommended by collection development librarians.

Creates, in consultation with appropriate members of the university community, policies concerning networked information issues including such issues as access, privacy, and security.

After initial implementation has been completed, assumes supervision and continued development of the IBM/CWRU Imaging System.

Serves as the primary contact representing the needs of the libraries serving Case Western Reserve University in campus planning for future computing and networking capability, working with other departments of Information Services and appropriate administrative and faculty groups.

Works with Information Network Services and other computing departments in order to network library technologies to broaden the access to information for campus researchers and to contribute local information and research findings to the larger academic and research communities.

Maintains effective relationships with vendors of library technology products.

Works with members of Information Services and other members of the university community to develop a collection of software appropriate to the needs of the institution.

Tests, implements, and supports new technologies related to the access of information on a variety of storage media and delivery mechanisms.

Represents CWRU on the national level in the work of appropriate research library associations and consortiums, such as the Coalition for Networked Information, as well as professional associations focusing on computing in higher education generally and research libraries specifically (e.g., EDUCOM, ASIS).

Develops proposals for fund raising and supervises activities on grant projects involving library technologies.

Qualifications:

Must have substantial knowledge of current library and information technologies and systems as well as emerging developments in the field and the potential requirements for meeting future information/library needs in a network environment.

A. Education
   MLS from an ALA-accredited institution or equivalent

B. Experience
   Seven years increasingly responsible professional experience in positions involved with the technological issues relevant to research libraries, including significant experience with local library systems and the issues related to providing access to information services on campus and national networks.

C. Other
   1. Proven analytical and problem-solving skills
   2. Strong organizational, interpersonal, and communication skills
   3. Demonstrated creativity and innovation in previous assignments
   4. Demonstrated initiative and commitment to making outside professional contributions

BEYOND SUBJECT ACCESS: THE NEXT GENERATION OF OPAC SOFTWARE

Mary Micco and Thomas Basista, Indiana University of Pennsylvania

Keywords: subject access, OPAC, expert systems, hypermedia, natural language mapping, graphical user interface, object-oriented programming, controlled vocabulary, relational database, Hypercard

Abstract: This research project has focused on using advanced technologies to improve subject access for online catalogs with particular emphasis on hypermedia to provide a friendly user interface. We found that there were two very different problems to be addressed to improve subject access. The first issue is the very large number of failed searches, upwards of 30 % even in very large online catalogs such as Melvyl. Numerous studies have evaluated the reasons for this very high failure rate. One of our project goals was to build a natural language mapping scheme that would lead the user from the term of choice such as World War II to the controlled vocabulary term World War, 1939-1945.
The second problem identified is that of unacceptably large sets retrieved when using the controlled vocabulary. The average number of items retrieved per search in Melvyl in one particular week was 171 items. There is no reason to believe this is atypical. Another major goal of our work has been to provide tools to enable users to effectively narrow down large retrieved sets. Inevitably the more sophisticated the number of search options the harder it is for users to understand. In this paper we will focus on the user interface design issues. We were succesful in merging several different technologies to achieve the desired flexibility. We combined a hypermedia front end with a relational database server while using an expert system to help guide and manage the search process. This prototype was developed on a Macintosh with Hypercard and Oracle.

1. GRAPHICAL USER INTERFACES

The user interface is defined as the interaction between the user and the computer in the performance of a given task Clearly in a task as complex as navigating the world of information resources, the design of the user interface will take on growing significance. At present the controversy rages over the comparative merits of graphical user interfaces (GUI) versus command driven ones (CUI). A recently completed study by Temple, Barker and Sloane(1990) confirms that most computer users prefer systems with a GUI to those they must control by typing in strings of commands. They also found that a GUI can raise productivity considerably. Overall, experienced GUI users finished 58 percent more correct work and and novice GUI users 48 percent more in the same time as their counterpart CUI users. In this paper we have focused on the problem of developing a GUI to support subject searching in on line catalogs. We have examined the processes involved as well as the many different skill levels of users approaching the OPAC. Then we have tried to design a user interface that supports this process effectively. This involved reevaluating traditional subject searching techniques. We now have a working prototype with 100,000 Marc records and have been able to test the performance of our system on both precision and recall as well as ease of use. We experienced many difficulties when we tried to develop subject clusters by linking Library of Congress Subject Headings (LCSH) with the appropriate Library of Congress classification numbers.

2. ICONS AS NAVIGATIONAL TOOLS

The most critical aspect of the user interface is that it should support the whole process in a way that is natural and yet structured. It should be easy to follow, easy to understand, easy to change and yet at the same time support the skilled searcher who does not need this kind of handholding. Expert users are easily accomodated by the standard method of providing command key combinations for the commonly used commands and putting these clearly in the menu options. More difficult is the problem of providing adequate navigation tools to assist novice users in moving about freely. We took advantage of Hypercard's ability to provide a standard set of buttons on every screen. For instance there is always a "Home" icon on every screen that lets you jump back to the initial entry screen from any point. There are also next screen and previous screen arrows. We decided that it would also be helpful to develop a set of 12 icons that would be used consistently throughout as navigation tools. The key to succesful design of a direct manipulation interface is that it should free the user to concentrate on learning the task not the system. With this in mind we studied the task of the searcher and much of the literature that has been written about it and identified a set of tasks that would be represented by icons.

2.1 Developing the User Profile

Our primary focus was on search by subject. We considered author, title and call number as known item searches requiring much less support. and will not discuss these options in this paper. The user selects the type of search desired by clicking on the appropriate icon.

Figure 1: Author, Title or Subject.

The user is taken to an input screen designed to support the activity selected. We have built in the ability to input a user profile that will guide the choice of materials to be presented. We would like to propose that reading level be used in subdividing large sets of materials. A reader can readily determine whether they want to see serious scholarly material written for the research community, technical material or only material written for the layman. If we are to succesfully develop a system that is somewhat intelligent and can support different user profiles then we will need to reevaluate the information being captured in the MARC record. At present there is a tag for intellectual level but it is not being used. Publishers are very clear about what market they are targetting and should be required to put this information in the cataloging data that eventually wends it way through the system. Our default is not to impose any restriction but to show all materials found.

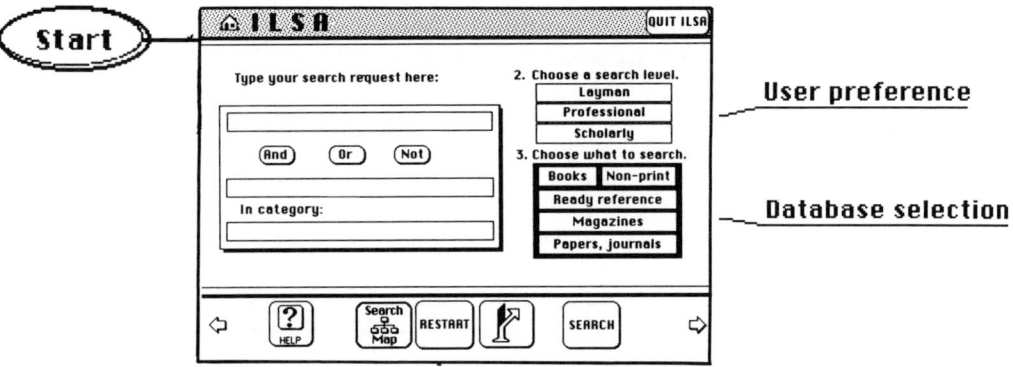

Figure 2. The Basic Input Screen.

2.2. Selecting the Database to Search

Next the user is asked to indicate what database they want to search. Given the present state of networking there is no reason why library search terminals caanot provide access to a wide variety of networked databases. To accomplish access to non-print we simply add a filter that checks the form of the material. For access to the ready reference collection we have currently Websters Dictionary and the Oxford book of Quotations but many others would be useful and desirable.

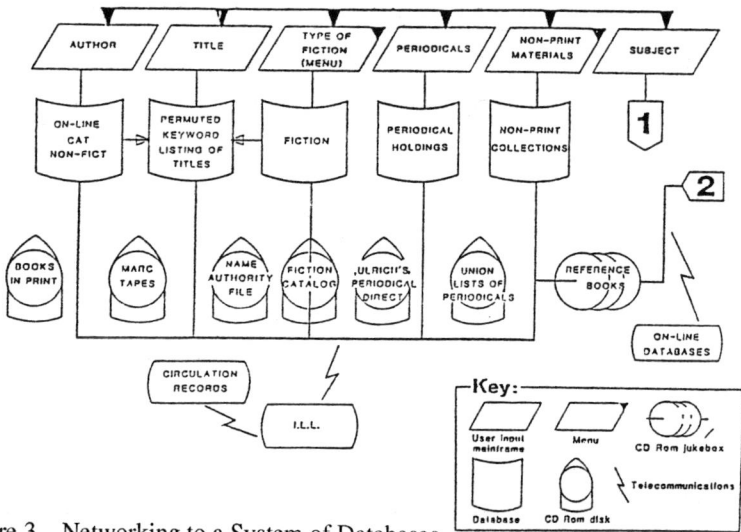

Figure 3. Networking to a System of Databases.

CD-Rom has provided the answer to making access to periodical databases cost effective at least on a small scale. We look forward to the day in the not very distant future, when a centralized CD-rom server will be able to support dial up access from all library terminals and be able to serve up a selection of CD-Roms efficiently and effectively.

2.3. Entering the Broad Subject Category of Interest

To improve our searches and obtain better results we also prompt the user to enter the broad subject category of interest. In our formative evaluation of this feature we have found that people often seek help. Our help screen for this is shown below in Figure 4. Our goal is to encourage users to select a broad category or class that can be used by the expert system to more accurately match the users interests with the material available e.g. Banks can be considered financial institutions but also are associated with marine life. The two broad categories might be described as Finance and Zoology and can be easily differentiated by class number, thereby improving the precision of the search. Conversely if nothing is found the broad subject category will provide the system with a starting place to suggest alternatives.

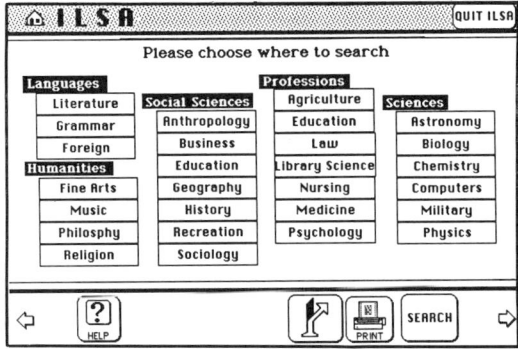

Figure 4: Narrowing the Subject.

3. AN EXPERT SYSTEM TO SUPPORT SEARCHING

Most of the present generation of OPACS return with the number of hits and abandon the user to his or her own devices. Yet studies done in large systems, and particularly the research done by Clifford Lynch at Melvyl, demonstrates that we are developing two very different problems requiring very different solutions. Dr. Lynch claims that in some weeks on Melvyl the number of failed search (those yielding 0 hits) exceeds 30%. This statistic strongly suggests that we need to provide help for failed searches. On the other end of the spectrum, the remaining 70 % too often find themselves wallowing in too many hits. The averages reported by Dr. Lynch in his weekly statistics range from 171 to over 260. In other words users are finding more than they want to deal with and need help in narrowing down these large retrieved sets. There is the additional problem that some headings have become so large that the user cannot access or view these hits at all.

To deal with this situation our prototype system was provided with an embryonic expert system that monitors the number of hits retrieved and takes appropriate remedial action when needed. We also made numerous modifications to the supporting software and indexing strategies. As shown in the simplified flow chart below, if the user finds nothing the expert system will go into expand mode and provide assistance to the user in expanding the search. If on the other hand, too much is returned then the system will go into the narrow search mode and will make appropriate suggestions. Otherwise the system will simply display the hits in the normal manner. The user can also elect to narrow or expand at will simply by clicking on the icon of choice.

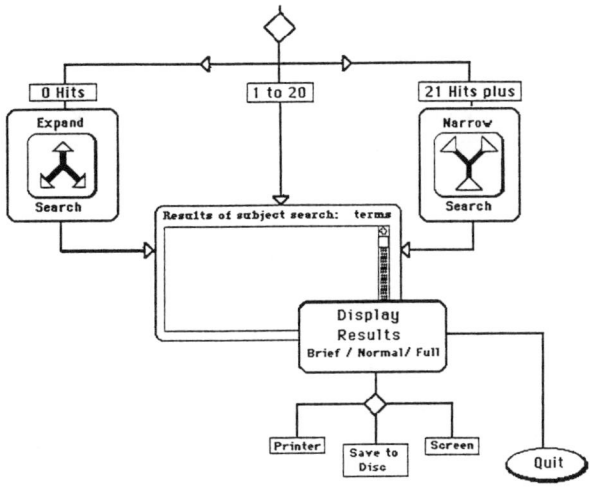

Figure 5: Flowchart of the system.

It is of course necessary to maintain a search history and we accomplished this by maintaining this data on a separate screen accessed by simply selecting the search map icon. While in this screen if the user selects the change search path icon they are immediately returned to the search entry screen to select a different database on the list displayed. . The users we have tested to date have had little difficulty in navigating with these icons We have made every effort to use them consistently and to place them where the most frequently used are most obvious..

Figure 6. Navigation Icons.

3.1 Expanding a Failed Search

The expert system drops into its expand mode whenever a very low number of hits is retrieved and will help the user to select from a number of options as shown in Figure 7. If the number of terms submitted as a string for searching is three or greater, it will suggest that the user retry with fewer terms. Another option is to check the spelling by dropping into Webster's Dictionary. A different possiblity is to use wildcarding. The user does not need to know the syntax for this but simply selects the option and the code will be generated for them automatically. After testing this option we found it necessary to refine it. The default is to look for an **exact match** on the term or phrase typed in. In the retrieved set we include all subdivisions, since many novice users do not realize they exist. e.g. war also retuns subheadings such as 'war--study and teaching'. The next level of expansion is a phrase that **begins wtih** the term selected such as 'war games'. If little is found the system will suggest searching for the term **anywhere** it appears, yielding phrases such as World War, 1939-1945. If the search is still failing, the user is directed to the explore topic option. This is our natural language mapping system that takes uncontrolled terms from wherever possible in the Marc record including notes, table of contents and titles and links these terms to the controlled vocabulary of the primary LCSH heading assigned to that work. In all we created over a million such natural language links in our system by a completely automated process.

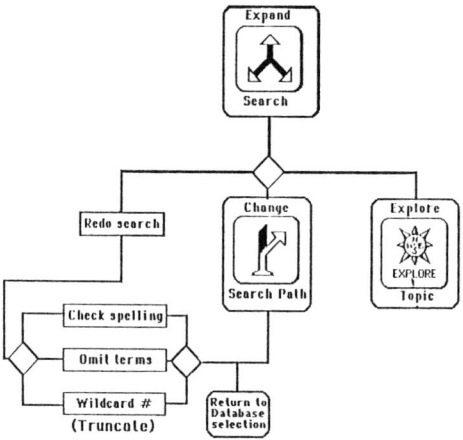

Figure 7. Expand the search.

An example of an explore topic search is shown below in Figure 8.
The searcher is looking for material on suicide. We have sorted the primary subject headings retrieved by class number to show the distribution better. Users also have an option to sort alphabetically by subject headings. Notice that the work suicide is missing from these subject headings. However the word suicide has appeared somewhere in the Marc record. What is being displayed is the first or primary subject heading assigned to the record in question as well as the class number for that book.

3.2 Narrowing Large retrieved sets.

Much more difficult is the problem of how to reduce a set that is too large without losing valuable data, particularly since the goal is to find the best of what is available and that involves value judgements.
   Dividing the database into three indexes.

One of the solutions we are currently testing is to divide up our keyword indexes into three files. The first file to be searched in response to a user query, is the set generated from the first subject heading assigned to each work. This heading, according to Mary Kay Pietris of the Library of Congress generally represents the aboutness of the book as a whole unit. If the search locates an entry in this database the user can be fairly confident that they have found whole books on their topic of interest. This index is not as large but if the user finds what

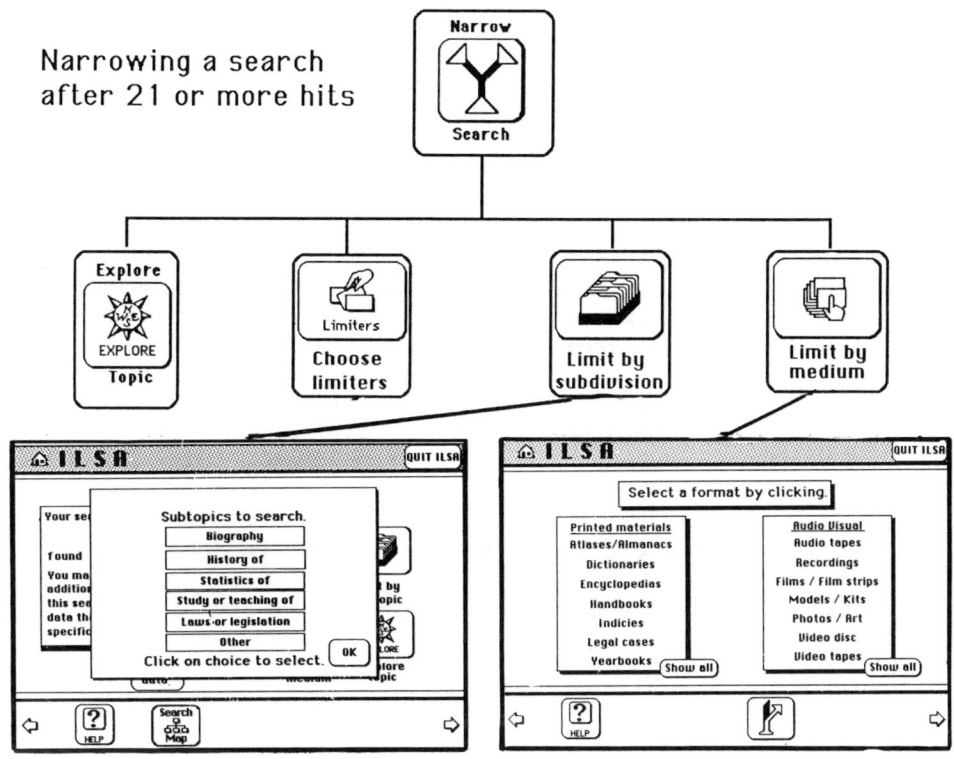

Figure 8. Options for Narrowing the Search..

they want here they are getting the best of what is available. At this point if they are still finding too many books the system can offer a variety of other strategies for narrowing large sets.

The second index file is built of keywords extracted from all other 6xx headings assigned to the book, a group which we refer to as secondary headings. If a book is found here it means that it contains some material on the topic but it is not its primary focus. Finally, in the third index file, we enter all other keywords associated with the book. This means there is some reference to the topic but not enough to warrant assigning a heading or the wrong term was selected and the user is being pointed back to the preferred terminology. Note that in all cases we display the primary heading and the class number for each book. We have also provided captions for the class numbers. Linking the subject headings to the class number assigned to the book is accomplished when the indexes are built. Obtaining the English captions for the headings proved rather more difficult. The Library of Congress Classification Schedules have not yet been automated and will require a lot of work before they can be distributed. We solved this problem by limiting ourselves to the captions found in the very brief outline of the classification schedules currently distributed by LC. In all we had 210 captions representing all the 1,2 and 3 letter combinations in the schedules. The results of such a search are shown in Figure 9.

The database searched by default for a user query is the index of primary subject headings.

At all times the users can click on the standard icons to broaden or narrow their search by switching to the index of their choice.

Number Of Matches Found: 49			
CALL NUMBER	SUBJECT HEADING	CLASSIFICATION	TITLES
B1475.H85	Ethics, Modern—18th Century	PHILOSOPHY/RELIGION:History/System	1
BF173.S78	Psychology, Pathological	Psychology	1
BF441.J79	Decision-Making	Psychology	1
CB430.L54	Civilization, Modern—1950-–Psychologic	History of civilization	1
D767.4.A46	World War, 1939-1945--Amphibious Ope	HISTORY (General)/TOPOGRAPHY	1
D792.J3	Japan--Nihon Kaigun Koku-Bu--Shimpu	HISTORY (General)/TOPOGRAPHY	1
D805.P7	World War, 1939-1945--Prisoners And Pr	HISTORY (General)/TOPOGRAPHY	1
D810.J4	Holocaust, Jewish 1939-1945	HISTORY (General)/TOPOGRAPHY	1
DD247.G67	Goring, Hermann–1893-1946–Death Anc	History/Germany	1
GN668.R45	Women—Melanesia--Congresses	Anthropology	1
HC59.B2513	Economic History--1945-	Economic history/conditions BY COUNT	1
HM22.F8	Durkheim, Emile–1858-1917	Sociology (General and theoretical)	1
HM51.J47	Sociology	Sociology (General and theoretical)	1
HM51.S634	Sociology	Sociology (General and theoretical)	1
HN15.E46	Social Problems	Social history/Social problems/reform	1
HQ196.P3	Prostitution--France–Paris--History--19tl	Family/Marriage/Women	1
HQ799.A8	Juvenile Delinquents—Australia	Family/Marriage/Women	1
ML2551.A8	One Hundred Thousand Australian Love	Literature of music	1
PK2211.E3	Urdu Poetry—20th Century—Translations	Indo-Iranian languages/lit	1
PN849.A952	Australian Literature--Women Authors	LITERATURE/history/collections	1

Figure 9. Explore Topic option: Search for suicide.

Limit by medium (form subdivisions).

One of the limiting options that our users have found particularly valuable is the list of 70 or so form subdivisions that our staff selected as being the most useful. Users can browse through this list and select from there or they can pick from the items shown. Note that we make a distinction between print and non-print materials. The code is generated for them, added to their search strategy and resubmitted.

Limit by subdivision (free floating subdivisions)

We extracted our subfields for x, y and z and generated three small browseable files that users could examine. The idea was that they would select the heading of their choice and the software would automatically add this limiter to their search strategy and resubmit. Along the way we encountered a number of problems. The x subdivisions follow no consistent pattern and are ofter very specific to the heading from which they were generated. So much so that they make little sense in a free standing list:. To avoid this problem and to reduce the length of the list to manageable proportions we decided to limit to a reasonable subset of the more commonly used subdivisions. A sample of these is shown above in figure 8.

Limit by Period or Place.

It seemed very reasonable to use the y and z fields as free standing browseable data bases but this too proved to be more difficult than we had anticipated. The geographic subdivisions are often very specific and leave one painfully aware of our very limited knowledge of geography, e.g. entries were found for 'Balonne Region','Chili River Watershed','Pottsville Region'.

The choronological divisions were never designed to sort chronologically and in fact defy any form of sorting. They do not follow any uniform format that we could detect. To solve this problem with a quick fix we went through the database by hand and coded an extra field for the start data of each period involved. e.g. 20th Century. ...1900; Age of tyrants, 7th - 6th centuries, B.C.... - 600. Having done this we were able to sort these fields by date and then conduct searches such as 'any material from 1000 B.C to the Birth of Christ' with the following results:

> Age of tyrants, 7th - 6th centuries. B.C.
> 510-30 B.C.
> Persian Wars, 500-449 B.C.
> Peloponnesian War, 431-404 B.C.
> Spartan and Theban Supremacies, 404-362 B.C.
> Warring states, 403-221 B.C.
> 324 B.C.-1000 A.D.
> B.C. -476 A.D.
> Roman period, 55 B.C. -449 A.D
> Empire, 30 B.C.
> The Five Julii, 30 B.C.-68 A.D.

Figure 9. Retrieving by Chronological Divisions.

Limit by Known Items (Author, Date, Title)

Another menu is presented where users can enter a known item such as an author, title or date of publication to limit the search. The option to limit by language is also offered. The user can freely choose as many options as they want and the code will be generated and added to their strategy, with the warning however that the more options you put in the less likely you are to find anything. We have not yet had an opportunity to obtain much feedback on these options which are still under development.

4. DESIGNING THE GRAPHICAL USER INTERFACE

ILSA, the system described in this paper is an information retrieval system designed to facilitate the task of finding information and displaying it. Throughout our project we have been concerned with using good graphic design and features to support the task at hand.

4.1 Screen Layout and Design

Galitz (1989) categorizes screen display functions into three basic types; data entry, such as those used for filling out a form or questionnaire; information retrieval, where data must be read from a screen; and combination screens, which have characteristics of both. Screens for data entry should be designed to allow easy left to right eye movement to facilitate data entry. Screens for information retrieval should allow rapid top to bottom scanning to minimize eye movements. Where both tasks are required, the design should favor the primary task.

While screen design is still more of an art than a science there are some objective measures such as screen complexity and text density that we did take into account.

We followed Galitz's advice that design elements such as blinking cursors, sound, reversed color text and colors while they may serve to attract a user's attention can quickly become distractions if used to excess.

4.2 Icon Design

Studies by Hutchins, et al (1985) stress the icons should resemble the functions and commands they are to represent as much as possible. It is also helpful if the icons are accompanied by verbal cues. (Petterson, 1980).
In all we developed 12 distinctive icons that were used consistently throughout the system as navigational tools. Each icon was assigned a particular destination and/or task to perform.

4.3 Overall Instructional Design.

There is a very real danger in supporting a complex task such as this one that the number of different screens will be overwhelming and the user will get lost in hyperspace. To prevent this from happening, we have tried to guarantee that the user will find material of interest or will be returned to the initial data entry screen in no more than 6 moves. It was also important to provide a great deal of navigational flexibility. We maintain a search history screen all the time where the user can revisit an earlier search. The expert system monitors the user's progress and will make helpful suggestions as the search progresses.

5. CONCLUSION

There are many new technologies available today which offer exciting possibilities for improving information retrieval in very large textual databases. Our research is progressing on two fronts. We have been looking at ways to improve vocabulary control (Alberico & Micco, 1990) but we have also been studying the importance of designing a good graphical user interface to support the task of the searcher.

This research is being supported by the Council on Library Resources and the Department of Education through a Library Technology Grant. Carlyle Systems Inc. has provided technical support and access to the source code fro the current TOMUS software.

BIBLIOGRAPHY

Alberico, Ralph & Mary Micco. Expert Systems for Reference and Information Retrieval. Westport, CT: Meckler Publishing Co, 1990.
Galitz, W.O. Handbook of Screen Format Design. 3rd. ed. Wesley, MA : QED Informational Services. 1989
Hutchins, E.L., et al. Direct Manipulation Interfaces. San Diego, CA: California University, LaJolla Institute for Cognitive Science , 1985 (ERIC Document Reproduction Service No. ED 261 655)
Lynch, Clifford , In Hudson, Judith and Walker, Geraldine. "The year's work in technical

LIBRARY AUTOMATION AND THE ADVENT OF THE KNOWLEDGE NETWORK

Todd Miller, Information Access Company

Keywords: Information; database; library automation; network; online; CD ROM

Abstract: This paper discusses a new trend in data distribution, "Knowledge Networking." This phrase is used to describe the distribution of data over wide-area networks on a site license basis. Typically, this information is made available via library automated online public access catalog (OPAC) systems. The geographical scope of this information offering is impressive; sites buying into this service range from individual library systems to multi-state library consortia with literally thousands of terminals tapped into the system. It is anticipated that Knowledge Networks will have a profound impact on the information industry, particularly on CD-ROM and traditional online.

1. Introduction

Before the victims of the last info-revolution are cold in their grave, a new upheaval is once again shaking up the information industry. The "Knowledge Network," a new trend in data distribution, is rapidly changing the face of the library community. Knowledge Networking describes the distribution of tape-based information via library automated systems. This form of data distribution is being pioneered by academic and public libraries, though there is little question that similar offerings will find their way into the corporate environment with an equally profound impact.

2. Implementation

At present, Knowledge Networks are being implemented in two basic ways. Both involve the access of magnetic tape-based information through the library's Online Public Access Catalog (OPAC) system, though they vary on where the data resides. One method houses the tapes locally at the library site; the second entails remote access of tapes stored offsite. The "look and feel" of these approaches is identical -- in both situations, the data is channeled through the library's OPAC search software, resulting in a uniform user interface for both the book catalog, as well as other databases. There are trade-offs to both approaches: the first involves a considerable investment in CPU, storage, and personnel resources required to load, process, and access the data; a library which adopts the second approach incurs telecommunication line lease charges and the cost of networking software.

3. "Harmonic Convergence"

Libraries are implementing Knowledge Networks at a remarkable pace, owing largely to a situation in which preparation, demand, opportunity, and even economic recession have met simultaneously, producing a sort of industry "harmonic convergence."

Preparation has manifested itself in the widescale installation of automated online public access catalog systems. Implementation of these systems in-effect represent the construction of the "physical highway" upon which intellectual commerce is transported, literally "paving the way" for the creation of the network. OPAC systems have developed rapidly in the United States. Today, over 41% of *all* libraries in the United States have implemented automated systems.

Demand for intellectual content in electronic form was established in dramatic fashion by the so-called "CD revolution" of the '80's which powerfully demonstrated the latent patron appetite for electronic information. Today, over 1,300 CD information products exist[1], with known installations in over 5,500 libraries. Online services such as Prodigy, Compuserve, and Dow Jones, which cater to the end user, are experiencing steady growth in usage as well.

Opportunity has taken the form of tape offerings from the three major electronic information publishers, Information Access Company, University Microfilms, and H.W. Wilson, all three of which have recognized the potential of site licensing for the library, the patron, and the vendor. At present, the lion's share of information offerings available are comprised of bibliographic citations to periodical literature, though this will undoubtedly expand over time.

Because the information publishers are liberated from supplying the vehicles for data delivery data, they can grant wide-area licenses at a much lower cost-per-terminal than would be the case with CD-ROM media. This allows libraries to offer significantly greater access to information without dramatically increasing expenditures. In addition to greater information supply, patrons benefit from consolidation of multiple information sources on single terminals. It is now possible to access monograph catalogs, indexes, abstracts, and full text to periodical literature, encyclopedic and directory information all from the same OPAC terminal, using the identical search and retrieval engine.

As if libraries didn't already have plenty of reasons to implement Knowledge Networks, the current recession provides even greater impetus, forcing libraries to find creative ways to provide the greatest degree of service at the lowest possible cost. An extension of this value mindset is the sudden increased involvement of consortia in Knowledge Networking. By banding together, large systems can pool technical and economic resources, driving their collective costs down, and winning reduced information subscription rates thanks to greater economies of scale.

The geographical scope of consortia is awesome. Sites buying into this service range from individual library systems to multi-state library consortia with literally thousands of terminals tapped into the network.

4. <u>Future Shock</u>

Given this extraordinary level of activity, it is not difficult to predict that Knowledge Networks will have a seismic effect on the information industry, with particular impact felt on CD-ROM. It is likely that CDs will be transplanted over time from mainstream general reference applications to highly specialized and archival functions. Additionally, CD ROM will tend to move from the large and mid-sized libraries to smaller libraries, which can not afford the high cost of buy-in for automated systems. Some automation vendors are experimenting with hybrid offerings which offer simultaneous access to both tape and CD file servers. This approach makes good sense, allowing libraries to offer uniform access to high-usage general purpose tape-based information, as well as low-usage vertical CD-based data.

Aftershocks of Knowledge Networking will not be limited to CD-ROM. It is likely that easy-to-use, fixed-price information access will entice corporate end users to this form of data retrieval. This will undoubtedly affect the traditional online world.

How the network will evolve in the future is not clear, though some intelligent guesses can be made. Widespread access to bibliographic data on the network will drive intellectual access to the source material to levels never before experienced, straining the library's ability to serve up this material from traditional sources. The next logical step will be the enabling of access to the source material itself through the net.

Complementing the periodical information offered on networks will be data from other sources, such as encyclopedias and directories.

As to where the Knowledge Network will ultimately transport libraries is also uncertain, although one possible future might look like this: Libraries will grow beyond their walls, offering an ever-increasing amount and variety of information through the network, including full text, images, and executable code. It is conceivable that as the library grows beyond walls and on the network, the librarian will go onto the network as well, offering online "operator" assistance in identifying the appropriate source for information, as well as assisting users in the construction of searches. In this way, the network may liberate the librarian from the role of information custodian, and reaffirm the role of information navigator.

Other information career opportunities may develop as the volume of information available through the network increases. Wading through the growing bank of data will undoubtedly become cumbersome, providing incentive for the development of Selective Dissemination Information (SDI) macro-searches. Certain rote searches, such as monitoring competition or market developments, may create a market for canned SDI's.

Although Knowledge Networking provides compelling new opportunities for libraries, it also creates new dilemmas. Faced with information now available in a dizzying array of media, the information professional must deal with a frightfully complex decision matrix, and must decide which materials are most appropriate for which medium. The librarian must decide what data will justify the cost of mounting on the net based on anticipated usage. Clearly, there is a point of diminishing returns both in terms of longevity and scope, beyond which the benefits of housing knowledge on the net is outweighed by the costs of storage and maintenance.

5. Conclusion

Considering the root of the word "revolution," it does seem appropriate to apply this word to the movement toward Knowledge Networking, given the fact that we are, in effect, returning to the big multiuser systems of the past as the means of accessing information. This is not to say that there is no place for CD-ROM in the future, quite the contrary. What it means is that we now have at our disposal a highly efficient and cost-effective way to broadcast general purpose information in wholesale fashion to an extremely large audience. This presents compelling new opportunities for the information professional, as

well as unknown new challenges. In spite of the intriguing
possible futures offered by the network, the anticipation
of these extraordinary changes may provoke some uneasiness
-- an understandable reaction when one is standing on
shaky ground.

6.   **References**

    1.   *CD-ROMs In Print*. Westport: Meckler
Publishing, 1990

CD-ROM AS BACKUP FOR ROCKWELL INTERNATIONAL'S RTIS/TECHLIB SYSTEM

Martha T. Mori, Rockwell International Corporation

Keywords: Backup Media, CD-ROM, Microfiche

Abstract: In 1987, when Rockwell International integrated the catalogs of six Technical Information Centers (TICs) onto a single online library system, the question of backups and alternative search methods -- how do you find things if the online system is down --emerged as an issue.

Printing listings on paper was discarded as impractical and too costly: the nineteen participating TICs (thirteen information centers joined the new system), spanned the continent and the 275,000+ catalog entries would have taken reams of paper to print and a fair expense to ship. Microfiche was considered as an option because it was compact and relatively cheap to produce. Lastly, CD-ROM technology was considered because CD's held enormous amounts of data on a single disc, and the technology provided a flexibility of access unavailable from both paper and microfiche.

Rockwell needed to compare the two backup media before making a decision as to which to use. This paper will present the results of that comparison. What does microfiche cost and what do you get? What does CD-ROM technology cost and what does it buy you? How would the TICs react to a change from microfiche to CD-ROM methods?

1. INTRODUCTION

With the advent of RTIS, the Rockwell Technical Information System, Rockwell was able to consolidate the catalogs of nineteen TICs (Technical Information Centers) and the TICs had online access to a corporate-wide catalog. A decision had to be made as to which backup media to use for this burgeoning data so that the catalog would be available during those times when the online inquiry system was unavailable.

2. MICROFICHE

Microfiche had played a large part in the old (pre-RTIS) catalog system. There were seven microfiche reports: catalog entries were indexed by Author, Catalog/ Accession No., Contract No., Corporate Source, Descriptive Terms, Document No., and Title. Monthly supplements and cumulative indexes were also a part of the microfiche backup system. Six Rockwell libraries participated in the old files, which were updated monthly by batch procedures. Each library had copies of the other five libraries' microfiche reports.

TIC library staff members' job responsibilities included microfiche filing and related functions, i.e., file monthly supplements and cumulative indexes, inventory the microfiche, and correct all user filing errors.

Preliminary plans were drawn to develop four microfiche reports (sorted by Author, Contract Number, Subject and Title). TECHLIB/BASIS profiles and reports were developed to write out all fields necessary to process all microfiche reports.

These reports would have required an annual database dump of all records from the RTIS database; the batch computer costs were estimated as $3,500 to dump the database and $3,000 in additional charges for monthly supplements and cumulative indexes.

Additional one-time charges would have been incurred for the development of application programs. A budget of $32,000 had been set aside for these reports, monthly supplements and cumulative indexes for the TICs.

Microfiche reader-printers were already installed at all TICs. If needed, replacement costs for reader-printers were estimated at $5,000.

3. CD-ROM

A little later inquiries were made into the costs and advantages of using CD-ROM rather than microfiche. CD-ROM's large storage capacity particularly interested the nineteen TICs, whose holdings included over 560,000 records or 275,000+ publications.

Hardware requirements consisted of an IBM PC XT/AT or compatible with 640K RAM, a floppy drive, 10 MB hard disk, monitor, CD-ROM player, and printer (optional). Additional required software was MS-DOS 3.1 or greater and Microsoft MS-DOS CD-ROM Extensions.

In 1988, CD-ROM players were estimated to run from $700-$900. In addition, the MS-DOS CD-ROM Extensions software was available with the CD-ROM player at the time of purchase.

An initial concern about changing to CD was that the librarians and their staffs would drastically decrease their use of the online system because the CD system would turn out to be easier to use and less expensive to operate. This would have made the librarians unfamiliar and uncomfortable with the system which was in fact required for the production of the CDs. Another consideration was that the smaller TICs might not be able to afford a PC and CD-ROM player.

A comparison of costs and search capabilities was made with hardware and software requirements and presented to the Rockwell TICs:

	CD-ROM (Complete File)	**MICROFICHE** (4 Reports)
TOTAL (Includes costs for application development and 4 issues)	$ 21,000.	$ 32,000.
(Cost per Quarterly reissues)	$ 5,250.	$ 3,300.*
Search Capabilities:		
Access Points	30	1 per Report
Boolean Operators	yes	none
Index Searches	yes	none
Query Results SAVE and RECALL	yes	none
Text Searches	yes	none

*With monthly microfiche supplements.

All but two TICs met the hardware and software requirements, except for the CD-ROM player.

With this information in hand, the Rockwell TICs selected the CD-ROM alternative. Vendor bids were then solicited in July, 1988. Three vendors contacted Rockwell and presentations and demonstrations were set up.

The TICs compared vendor products. Both a window query and profile query search systems were demonstrated at Rockwell. One window query system had particularly clear screen formats and was easy to use. The profile query system also had good screens and its software was able to search the entire catalog (all fields at the same time) for any specified character string.

Rockwell made its final choice based on costs, turnaround time for CD production, and, to some extent, extended capabilities available in the system finally chosen. Rockwell decided to purchase the CD-ROM product from EBSCO Electronic Information Division. With the remainder of the budget set aside for the development of microfiche reports, 16 CD-ROM players were purchased and distributed to the TICs.

A profile, report and supporting JCL were developed to create tape dumps of over 550,000 catalog and circulation records. Four tapes were required to hold the data that would reside on a single CD.

The first RTIS CD-ROMs were released to the TICs on September 29, 1988.

4. CONCLUSION

Since the first release of the CD, Rockwell TICs have been pleased with the CD and CD updates have been increased to bimonthly issues. Also, CDs have increased online data entry activities because TICs have been interested in adding their retrospective library holdings and having them appear on the CDs. One TIC noticed a significant decrease in their computer connect time to the mainframe because engineers used the CD for their searching activities. Engineers and staff members find RTIS CD-ROM easy to use and can also either print or download their result sets to floppy discs.

TICs no longer use staff time to maintain the backup system. In addition, because of newly acquired CD-ROM products, TICs are able to use their CD-ROM players with other CDs.

One Rockwell TIC was able to set up RTIS CD-ROM at a remote site and Rockwell engineers were able to access catalog data offline. The number of Rockwell TICs and remote sites requiring RTIS CD-ROMs has increased by 60% since the original CDs were sent in 1988.

The CD-ROM system has not been without its minor drawbacks. One limitation in the system chosen is that catalog records cannot exceed 5,000 characters in length. Another is that Circulation Item Lists, which link catalog records to circulation records, cannot exceed forty entries.

But, all in all, the CD-ROM system installed at the TICs is very easy to use, relatively inexpensive, and is a success at Rockwell International.

5. REFERENCE

1. Landau, Herbert B. Microform vs. CD-ROM: Is There A Difference? Library Journal 115, No. 16, p. 56-59, 1990.

SATISFACTION AND DISSATISFACTION WITH IOLS HARDWARE

Lester J. Pourciau, Memphis State University

Keywords: IOLS Hardware, Hardware Reliability, Hardware Obsolescence

Abstract: Throughout the twenty-five to thirty year experience of libraries with using computer technology to simplify routines and to enhance services, major advances have been made in system software, and in the capabilities that increasingly sophisticated system software offers. The one central factor in all of this experience has been computer hardware. This paper reports on user satisfaction and dissatisfaction with computer hardware used in integrated online library systems. It employs a content analysis technique applied to letters from various library directors and systems librarians about their experiences with IOLS computer hardware.

1. INTRODUCTION

The labor intensive nature of much of the work that is required to make libraries function effectively has long motivated librarians to seek applications of technology to their efforts. The one dominant piece of technology which has played the major role in the mechanization or the automation of library routines and procedures is the computer. Not only did the computer make much more efficient many library routines, procedures, and operations, but also in very recent years, it has played a very distinctive role in resource sharing as a result of networking developments and capabilities. In the early to mid-1970s, the first so-called turnkey library automation systems became available and throughout the latter part of the 1970s and into the 1980s, a major increase in the number of these systems became evident in any review of library automation in the United States (Ref.1). As system software became, and continues to become, increasingly sophisticated, so have hardware requirements become more demanding. Various libraries have been forced to upgrade hardware dramatically or, in other cases, even to abandon some given turnkey system and to adopt another with computer hardware being a major criterion on which a decision to change was based. A paper presented at the 14th International Online Information Meeting in December of 1990 (Ref. 2) was based on a questionnaire designed to elicit reasons why various libraries in the United States changed from one automated system vendor to another. One of the questions included in the questionnaire asked about obsolescence of computer hardware. This particular question evoked one of the stronger responses received. This present paper reports on a more detailed investigation of library satisfaction and dissatisfaction with IOLS hardware. An appendix to this paper includes a reproduction of the questionnaire results received as a result of the study mentioned above.

Question seven on the questionnaire is the particular one which asks about computer hardware. So as to obtain an elaboration and discussion of this particular reason, a letter was written to all of those libraries which reported having changed automation system vendor because of obsolete hardware that could not support current or projected system demand. It asked in an open-ended manner for any comment about maintenance cost, hardware reliability, vendor support, hardware adaptability, and other factors which might have been germane to system performance.

2. DISCUSSION OF RESPONSES

A number of different responses were received and, as might be expected, they varied a great deal in terms of their length, their specificity, and their discussion of hardware related problems. One or two of the responses were so general, or vague, as to yield no interesting comment about hardware reliability, but others were very specific, detailed, and very generous in their comment. What will follow here is the result of a content analysis technique of sorts used so as to extract, to identify, and to group various reasons for dissatisfaction as cited in responses received to the initial inquiry. So as to maintain anonymity on the part of those individuals who generously responded to this survey, no effort will be made to identify institutions, libraries, vendors, or particular hardware manufacturers. It should be clear as this discussion evolves that such anonymity will not detract from the identification of satisfaction or dissatisfaction with IOLS hardware.

One of the more interesting comments made by a respondent characterized librarians of the 1960s and 1970s as tending to believe that library automation could be treated like good typewriters. It could be bought, all of the squeaking parts could be oiled, and it would run forever. Further, this writer pointed out the unfortunateness of those librarians not being visionaries, and thinking only in terms of automating clerical tasks. These librarians were unable to see the major advances in information technology, transfer, handling, and networking that lay only a decade ahead. Here, though, we must remember the dictum of the physicist, Niels Bohr, who once offered the view that prediction about anything is difficult; especially about the future.

Specific reasons offered by various respondents about hardware dissatisfaction can be grouped under four general headings. The first of these is hardware reliability; the second is vendor support; the third is hardware adaptability; and the fourth is maintenance cost. Each of these, except for one facet of maintenance cost which will be discussed later, can be related to the age of the hardware. Several respondents commented that hardware life cycles tend to be increasingly shorter, and several offered the judgment that this shortened life cycle is planned by hardware manufacturers so as to continually have a new product to offer to potential customers. Typical hardware life spans as estimated by several of the respondents ranged from five to nine years with most comment settling on a six to seven year hardware life span. This stands in stark contrast to the comment identified above to the effect that many librarians of the '60s and '70s felt that a good library automation system well maintained would last forever.

Comments about vendor support are a curious mix of complaints about vendors altering equipment so as to make it non-standard and thus ensuring that the individual library seeks repair and maintenance from the vendor which sold the equipment associated with a system. Other complaints about equipment speak of rising maintenance costs charged by various vendors because of older equipment for which replacement parts tend to become scarce, and for which some replacement parts can be obtained only in the form of refurbished or remanufactured parts.

Paraphrases from each of the letters received will be listed below as they relate to each specific reason mentioned above:

Hardware reliability

Our first mainframe was almost seven years old and had experienced numerous power hits, was very sensitive to heat and power surges, and was thus causing us more down time.

As the equipment aged, it became increasingly difficult to get parts, and we experienced increasing down time.

Our field engineer was replaced by someone who had never become acquainted with the repair of our "antique" machines. These older machines required increasingly frequent repair.

Maintenance costs rose as the equipment aged until the cost/productivity ratio was very unfavorable.

There was nothing wrong with the system or the hardware at the time of purchase. The reason problems were encountered later is that nothing was done to upgrade the system between 1974 and 1986.

Vendor support

The city chose not to upgrade our operating system software, and the vendor became increasingly reluctant to do more to keep the system running.

As our system aged, the equipment required more frequent service, and parts were becoming difficult to secure.

The vendor claims to be losing money because of the increased amount of required service, and the increased cost of obtaining scare and obsolete parts.

Our contract required that terminals supplied by the original vendor had to be shipped cross-country to be repaired. This was an inconvenience for the staff and, at times, impaired our service.

. . . altered the hardware, making it non-standard, and therefore requiring . . . specialized maintenance.

Our geographical location meant that any downtime which required hardware maintenance would be at least nine hours in duration.

Maintenance costs rose as the equipment aged until the cost/productivity ratio was unfavorable.

Hardware adaptability

Our mainframe was unable to run the latest release of software and, given its reliability, we didn't want our software on it.

The mainframe could not support later releases of our operating system which would enable . . . the circulation system to perform at a greater level of capability.

The system was designed for circulation only. When we began to look for a system which included OPACs, acquisitions and other features, the jointly-owned equipment did not have the capacity to add the features we desired.

Changes in the industry seem intentionally directed toward short term usage of equipment in a never-ending cycle of new purchases.

We had outgrown our initial hardware and could no longer take advantage of our software maintenance contract since the updates could not be mounted on our six-year-old CPU.

Our concerns with the . . . were its outdated . . . operating system and age rather than reliability. We were interested in upgrading to a faster machine of more current vintage that could be clustered with the five other . . . machines on campus.

The main reason for abandoning the hardware was that there was no available hardware migration that would support our continued growth.

As more devices were added to the . . . system, response time began to degrade until it reached a completely unacceptable level. Hardware upgrade would have entailed major expenditures.

Maintenance costs

Maintenance costs kept increasing, and maintenance efforts became more difficult and increasingly unsuccessful.

As our equipment aged, and as it became more difficult to get parts, cost for these parts and thus cost for maintenance rose.

Our older equipment was requiring more frequent service and parts were becoming more difficult to secure and were becoming more expensive.

Field engineer claimed that the cost of replacement parts had risen dramatically because of their scarcity.

Our maintenance costs had become astronomical.

Altered hardware requiring specialized maintenance cost us more than it otherwise should have.

Maintenance costs rose as the equipment aged.

In several of the responses received, there were some hardware issues cited which really have nothing to do with reliability, adaptability, maintenance, or vendor support. These have primarily to do with hardware being unable to accommodate an operating system adopted by a library's parent organization. One respondent spoke to the desire to adopt a university-wide common platform so as to take advantage of local area network capabilities.

3. SOME CONCLUSIONS, OR LESSONS LEARNED

This paper has been a report on an effort to determine some specifics about reasons for satisfaction or dissatisfaction with IOLS hardware. Many of the reasons cited by individuals who responded to this writer's inquiry about their hardware experiences are not really surprising but, with some consistency, confirm what knowledgeable people already know. To confirm something known is, however, not necessarily a wasted exercise for it firms up a base for planning for future development. One of the writers who spoke about equipment being designed for short term use before replacement went on to suggest that the individual customer has very little, if any, control at all over the general movement of the computer industry. It takes but a moment's reflection to realize how true this statement really is. As one stops to acknowledge the size and magnitude of the computer industry on a global scale, there is a forced realization that the library facet of this huge market is relatively small and fairly crowded with vendors all grappling to maintain some market share. In order to do this they must, of course, try all kinds of techniques which include continually offering bigger and better things to customers. This clearly has an impact on what hardware libraries can originally afford, and what hardware they can afford to dispense with after limited periods of time. To be sure, the IOLS environment, including all of the networking capabilities which grow and increase almost on a daily basis, changes and expands rapidly. In light of this, it would behoove all persons involved in the selection of systems, or system components, or hardware for systems to look very carefully at hardware specifications so as to ensure that any hardware offered by a vendor is standard, off-the-shelf, and unmodified. The respondent identified earlier in this paper who characterized librarians of the 1960s and the 1970s as viewing automation in the same way that they viewed typewriters went further to suggest that librarians were not the only ones who should be chastised for not being computer visionaries. This respondent suggested that automation vendors also should also be faulted for tampering with computer hardware.

As the writer paraphrased above suggested, the only way libraries are going to avoid escaping hardware obsolescence problems is to apply long range planning and forecasting to library automation in the same way that it is applied to other library services. To be sure, this is easier said than done because of the constant state of flux of the computer industry and the rapid introduction of new machines in cycles of less than a year.

4. REFERENCES

1. Epstein, Susan Baerg. "Managing Technology." *Library Journal*, v. 115, pp. 100-101, December 1990.

2. Pourciau, Lester J. "Changing Partners: Factors Associated with Automated System Change in the United States." Online 90 Information, 14th International Online Information Meeting, *Proceedings*, pp. 479-484, December 1990.

APPENDIX 1

CHANGING PARTNERS: FACTORS ASSOCIATED WITH AUTOMATED SYSTEM CHANGE BY LIBRARIES IN THE UNITED STATES

QUESTIONNAIRE

1. Our library __70__ has, __54__ has not changed vendors since first purchasing an automated system.

    (If you checked "has not" above, please stop and return the questionnaire.)

Please mark all of those reasons which resulted in a decision on the part of your library to change from one system and vendor to another. Use a 1, 2, or 3 to indicate the gravity or importance of the reason with 1 being the least and 3 the greatest.

   *X   1   2   3

2. __1   19   5   3__ Incomplete and/or inadequate documentation.
   **MWA = 1.41

3. __1   17   7   14__ Inadequate telephone support for hardware and/or software
    MWA = 1.92   problems.

4. __2   9   11   19__ Unresolved system problems that remain unresolved for extended
    MWA = 2.26   periods of time.

5. __1   12   14   11__ Excessive down time due to slow vendor response to reported
    MWA = 1.97   problems.

6. __2   13   11   12__ Unacceptably long system response times during peak usage.
    MWA = 1.64

7. __2   1   8   34__ Obsolete hardware that cannot support current or projected
    MWA = 2.77   system demands.

8. __1   9   15   9__ Poorly designed software modules.
    MWA = 2.0

9. __1   14   7   8__ Software modules that consistently exhibit poor response
    MWA = 1.79   times.

10. __2   14   8   5__ Lack of industry standard connectivity software.
    MWA = 1.67

11. __   14   8   1__ Lack of help screens for staff and patrons.
    MWA = 1.43

12. __4   11   11   27__ A lack of confidence in the current vendor's future
    MWA = 2.33   performance.

   * Respondents did not use rating scale; not included in mean score.
   ** Mean weight assigned.

APPENDIX 1, Page 2

```
        *X    1    2    3
```

13.   <u>2   13   9   8</u> Rising costs disproportionate to enhancement or support.
      **MWA = 1.83

14.   <u>1   7   9   11</u> Abandonment of system by vendor.
      MWA = 2.15

15.   <u>2   15   6   10</u> Vendor's failure to meet software-release target dates.
      MWA = 1.84

16.   <u>1   12   12   8</u> Vendor inability to meet legally or informally specified
      MWA = 1.88   system-enhancement expectations.

17.   <u>1   16   10   3</u> Disagreement with vendor's expressed or manifest priorities.
      MWA = 1.55

18.   <u>2   10   4   10</u> Vendor's lapse into bankruptcy or its exit from the
      MWA = 2.0   marketplace.

19.   Environmental shift vis-a-vis the library, e.g.:

  a. <u>1   7   7   13</u> A new emphasis upon networking at the institutional level.
      MWA = 2.22

  b. <u>   13   6   5</u> A renewed or changed commitment to a particular system vendor
      MWA = 1.67   at the institutional level.

  c. <u>   9   8   11</u> An altered commitment by the institution to the library
      MWA = 2.07   (e.g., in the area of funding, or in Computer Center
                         support of the library's system).

  d. <u>2   3   6   23</u> An increasing sense by the library of the advanced age or
      MWA = 2.63   dysfunctionality of its system in relation to the
                         institution's system.

  e. <u>2   14   2   1</u> A system purchase decision made by the library's larger
      MWA = 1.11   formal or informal consortium of colleague libraries,
                         particularly when inter-library cooperation has been a
                         topic of discussion.

20.   <u>1   10   17   21</u> Attractiveness of new products offered by other vendors.
      MWA = 2.23

21.   <u>2   11   6   9</u> An institutional demand that the library acquire a system
      MWA = 1.92   with a specific capability, e.g., sophisticated
                         networking.

22.   <u>1   13   10   15</u> User complaints about system performance.
      MWA = 2.05

23.   <u>   15   3   4</u> Attractive financial offer from one or more vendors to adopt
      MWA = 1.50   that vendor's system.

  * Respondents did not use rating scale; not included in mean score.
 ** Mean weight assigned.

ACADEMIC LIBRARIES AND ACADEMIC COMPUTER CENTERS: UNITED WE STAND; DIVIDED WE FALL

Pal V. Rao, Central Missouri State University

ABSTRACT:

Economic, political, sociological and technological factors which seem to be shaping the collaborative efforts between academic computer specialists and academic librarians, are outlined. Some cooperative efforts which benefit both professions are identified.

Academic Libraries and Academic Computer Centers: United We Stand; Divided We Fall

The purpose of this paper is to explore some mutually beneficial avenues of cooperation between libraries and computer centers. It is not intended to discuss the relative merits of the different organizational structures of information services that are in use and that are being proposed for the various American University campuses. The relative opportunities and problems associated with each type of organizational structure to manage information services have already been documented by Molholt (1), Neff (2), Dougherty (3), and Woodsworth (4).

The focus here is to examine various factors which are going to shape the future of these two professions and identify some cooperative ventures that might benefit both professions. A variety of cooperative efforts can be undertaken by academic libraries and academic computer centers regardless of the administrative structure employed to manage them. The cooperative ventures can take place whether the academic library and the academic computer center report to the same manager or report to different managers.

Libraries and computer centers basically make resources available to their clients. In making these resources available, they take different approaches and practice different philosophies. For example, computer specialists usually give clients what they want or tell the clients that it cannot be done (a result of binary conditioning I suppose). Librarians on the other hand negotiate with the clients and help the clients to identify the resources needed; and if the identified resources are not readily available, suggest alternate ways of acquiring them. Compared to librarians, computer specialists have a clearly defined framework within which they try to provide services; and when a request falls outside of that framework, computer specialists do not hesitate to refuse the service. Librarians usually try to provide as many services as possible without paying too much attention to the operational framework.

The above deceptively simple observations indicate that both professions can benefit by working in a cooperative mode and by learning from each other. At the present time, on many campuses the management of all information resources is being consolidated under a single administrator. Such realignments make it possible for librarians and computer specialists to work in a more cooperative mode and become more comprehensive information services professionals. Even on the campuses where the library and the computer center fall under the jurisdiction of different vice presidents, librarians and computer specialists will have to undertake more collaborative efforts to meet the information services demands placed on them by their campus constituencies.

We are living in a continuously changing world. As someone once said, nothing in this world is permanent but change. According to H.G. Wells, the well known British author who wrote such classics as <u>Time Machine</u> and <u>War of the Worlds</u>, social, economic, political and technological factors are four major underlying factors that precipitate change. Let us examine these four factors within the context of library and computer services professional environments.

SOCIOLOGICAL FACTORS:

It has been estimated that an average American spends 3000 hours a year in media consumption as opposed to 400 hours per year devoted to reading. Given this scenario, libraries must adapt their information dissemination strategies from primarily a print medium to other media. In this adaptation of change librarians will have to depend and work with computer and media services professionals.

Academic librarians in general maintain good faculty relations, have an academic orientation, and in typical academic sense pay no attention to the bottom line. Academic librarians are concerned with breaking barriers that inhibit the free flow of information. Since they acquire their information resources from external sources, academic librarians are limited in their ability to provide service to what information the external sources can supply and to what information manipulation the external sources can provide.

Academic computer specialists usually have better relations with the campus administrative staff, tend to have business orientation, pay attention to cost effectiveness, and are oriented towards providing controlled access to information. They are also concerned with analyzing and developing information that meets local needs, have extensive data manipulation capabilities, and can generate very customized reports to meet specific conditions.

We are living in an age where information is doubling every twenty months. Remember months, not years, prior to 1990, we used to say that information is doubling every so many years, but not anymore. Not only the quantity, but the media on which the information is recorded is also increasing. On occasion one medium may gradually replace another medium. For example, eight track tapes were replaced by audio cassettes. More often than not a new medium creates a new constituency and finds a niche in the media market. On the whole, we have more information media (audio, video, print, etc.) and more formats (compact disc, digital audio cassette tapes, VHS, fax journals, etc.)

According to Woodsworth, the rising client expectations are another sociological factor that is calling for greater cooperation between libraries and computer centers (4). As the use of the personal computer by the academic community increases, the faculty, staff, and students are asking for services such as twenty-four hour access to online catalogs and other databases or being able to check out or renew materials from their personal computers. These services require a greater collaboration between libraries and computer centers.

Cimbala (5) points out another important sociological factor which is how each profession perceives the other. Computer folks don't want to be called librarians and librarians want to cling to their quasi faculty status. Perhaps this image problem associated with nomenclature may be overcome by calling both information services professionals.

POLITICAL FACTORS:

Librarians, through their academic orientation and faculty status, usually tend to be more connected into the campus political environment. Perhaps the computer center can benefit from such political support. In American politics, libraries come very close to motherhood and apple pie. No politician publicly opposes libraries and in recent times politicians seem to be associating educational quality with technology. Consequently libraries and computer centers together may fare better in funding requests than on a separate basis.

ECONOMIC FACTORS:

The information age economics heavily depends on the information literacy of its work force. An "information literate" person has the ability to extract relevant information from all information sources. In developing an information literate work force, libraries and computer centers will have to work in a collaborative mode as skills from both fields are essential for good information literacy.

Realizing the need for information literacy, some library schools have already incorporated computer and media courses into their curriculum. At some schools one has a choice of taking information science courses which are usually cross listed with the computer science curriculum. Some computer science departments have started developing and offering courses in information management.

At the present time there is high demand for information technology professionals who are knowledgeable in all areas. The demand is especially high for management personnel who have the vision and ability to unify computer, media, and library professional groups into a cohesive working group. Profit oriented information utilities are creating stiff competition for the services usually provided by the academic libraries and computer centers. For example, some of the papers presented at the 1990 EDUCOM annual conference were made available online to the users of ISAAC (an IBM supported information utility for the educators) the same day the papers presented at the conference. To meet the demands created by the above economic and market factors, librarians and computer specialists will have to undertake more collaborative efforts.

TECHNOLOGICAL FACTORS:

Telecommunications developments such as the Integrated Services Digital Network (ISDN) will enhance telecommunications delivery capacity to transmit entire books and TV picture images in a timely manner. To provide services in such a high tech environment, librarians, computer specialists, and media specialists need to fully cooperate and augment each others capabilities. For example, librarians are known for their abilities to organize information resources; computer specialists are known for developing delivery systems; and media specialists are known for promotion and training activities. Perhaps all these three professions can merge into a single profession known as Information Services Professionals. At least their respective professional associations seem to have recognized this possibility and have started establishing guidelines for cooperative ventures. For example ARL/CAUSE/EDUCOM guidelines for cooperative ventures are in draft stages.

Even the bottom line oriented private industry seems to have recognized the need for greater understanding and cooperation between libraries and computer centers. For example IBM organized and sponsored an event known as INFORMA in Austin, Texas in 1990 and is again planning on having one in April 1991 in Long Beach, California. The INFORMA is a forum designed for invited library and computer center administrators to discuss mutual collaborative efforts.

The Federal government through its grant programs and through such efforts as the National Research and Education Network (NREN) is creating an environment which calls for greater cooperation between library and computer professionals. For example, the NREN can be looked at as a vast plumbing system through which information flows. The development and maintenance of the plumbing system fall within the domain of the computer specialist. The selection and organization of information for flow through the system fall within the domain of the librarian. Consequently, to accomplish its objectives the NREN needs computer specialists as well as librarians.

Many recent developments on the American campuses also seem to be conducive for a greater degree of collaborative efforts between computer specialists and librarians. Let us examine some of these developments. The ubiquitous microcomputer on campus shifted processing from mainframes to microcomputers. As more and more applications began to move from the mainframe to distributed computing based on microcomputers, initially such moves were welcomed by the academic computer specialists as a way of eliminating the applications on backlog. More recently though the computer specialists find that too many applications have migrated from the mainframes, and there is realization in some academic computer centers that they need more applications to justify the expensive hardware. Consequently, they are eager to work with librarians in developing applications such as online Public Access Catalogs. Another development that is calling for increased cooperation is the relatively new phenomenon known as the local mounting of databases. Here we have come full circle. As machine readable databases such as Educational Resources Information Center (ERIC) tapes became available, some institutions developed local information retrieval systems to access the data on ERIC tapes (6). Gradually such systems gave way as Centralized Online Information Retrieval Systems such as DIALOG and BRS became available. With the introduction of CD-ROM technology, libraries moved away somewhat from the centralized services to CD-ROM in-house search stations. The latest trend seems to be moving away from microcomputer based CD-ROM search stations to mainframe based databases and search stations.

At present some academic libraries seem to be shifting back to the local mounting of databases on their campus mainframes using the software developed by such library automation vendors as BRS Technologies and NOTIS. The locally mounted databases are made available through the campus communications networks. As this local mounting of databases spreads through the academic campuses, it will necessitate a greater collaborative working relationship between computer specialists and librarians. Bibliographic and numeric databases often contain the non-standard ASCII characters. Computer specialists need to develop special computer programs to display all such non-standard characters. Without this specialized help librarians may not be able to display all the data in the databases. Once the faculty and staff start using these locally available bibliographic and numeric databases, the computer cnter may be expected to provide institutional databases such as course files and student records in a compatible format. The locally mounted databases not only add utility to the campus mainframe, but also provide additional opportunities for both professions to practice their unique skills which are information systems development and information retrieval.

In spite of the pressure created by various factors to work together, librarians and computer specialists will eventually work together because they want to, not because they have to. They both can benefit from each other's professional strengths. Computer specialists are usually concerned with developing systems that collect data, manipulate it and provide answers to specific questions. They tend to be transaction oriented. Librarians tend to be process oriented in that they search for interrelations among existing data to provide answers to client's complex questions. Librarians are expert information navigators. They understand their clients information seeking habits. Perhaps they can equip computer specialists with some of these skills. Similarly, computer specialists are well adapted to changing work environments. Librarians tend to be process and procedure oriented. Many of them shun change. However, the recent technological developments are continuously changing the librarian's work environment. Perhaps librarians can learn how to manage rapidly changing work environments from computer specialists.

Librarians and computer specialists working together can develop, implement, and offer better information services and products than can be done by either profession on a separate basis. They both will come to realize that it is in the interest of both professions to cooperate with each other. They will realize that if they do not cooperate with each other, the information utilities such as CompuServe will expand their services and provide stiff competition for libraries and computer centers (7). It is hoped by working together librarians and computer specialists will be able to meet the competition and will live up to the challenging times ahead.

1. Molholt, Pat. On Converging Paths: The Computing Center and the Library. The Journal of Academic Librarianship, 11, p. 284-285, November 1985.

2. Neff, Raymond K. Merging Libraries and Computer Centers: Manifest Destiny or Manifestly Deranged. EDUCOM Bulletin, 20, p. 8-12, Winter 1985.

3. Dougherty, Richard M. Libraries and Computing Centers: A Blueprint for Collaboration. College & Research Libraries, 49, p. 289-286, July 1987.

4. Woodsworth, Anne. Computing Centers and Libraries as Cohorts: Exploiting Mutual Strengths. Journal of Library Administration, 9, No. 4, p. 21-34, 1988.

5. Cimbala, Diane J. The Scholarly Information Center: An Organizational Model. College & Research Libraries, 48, p.393-398, September, 1987.

6. Rao, Pal V. ERIC Data Access System (EDAS). Charleston, IL: Eastern Illinois University, 1979. (ERIC Document Reproduction Service No. ED 168 504).

7. Rao, Pal V. and Rao, Laura M. An Overview of Information Utilities. Information Executive, 4, No. 1, p. 12-14, Winter 1991.

LIBRARY NETWORKING IN VERMONT: AN ANALYSIS OF USAGE PATTERNS AND COST-EFFECTIVENESS

Jeffrey R. Rehbach, Middlebury College

The library catalogs of the Vermont Department of Libraries, the Vermont State College campuses, Middlebury College, Norwich University and the University of Vermont have been linked via a statewide network. The online catalogs use Data Research and NOTIS software. Telecommunications linkages among the library systems utilize leased telephone lines and the state microwave system. Many smaller public, school and academic libraries in the state have dialin access to the network. Preliminary investigation, based on data drawn from transaction logs and a survey of library staff to whom the network is available, reveals that network usage is highly variable, with significant differences among academic and public libraries' and their patrons' uses of the system. Cost-effectiveness of the network is evaluated on the basis of value-added services, and projected network enhancements are outlined.

The Vermont Automated Library System (VALS) comprises the linked library catalogs of the Vermont Department of Libraries (DOL), the Vermont State Colleges, the University of Vermont (UVM), Middlebury College, and Norwich University. NOTIS software is used at UVM, while Data Research (DRA) systems are in place at the other libraries.

The library catalogs are linked in two different ways. Data Research's online catalog software permits remote DRA catalogs to be searched from the local site's catalog, using commands as if the user were searching the local system; for example, a user at one of the State Colleges can select Middlebury from a menu within the online catalog program; a link to the Middlebury is established, and the user proceeds to search the Middlebury catalog with screen displays that have been designed by the State College systems managers, not by Middlebury. In contrast, the link to and from UVM is not as integrated; DRA users select an information gateway menu option for the UVM catalog, and are connected to an available port at UVM, from which they use the NOTIS system as if they were UVM users. At UVM, just two terminals in the library, as well as the main data switch on campus, are linked to the Department of Libraries, whereby a menu selection offers access to any of the Vermont DRA sites. Several of the DRA sites provide additional frontend menu options for displaying information files on their systems.

Telecommunications linkages among the locations utilize a combination of leased lines and microwave. Terminals at five regional libraries are linked to the state library in Montpelier via multiplexors running over leased phone lines. Some 125 public, school and small academic (independent of the state college system) libraries with microcomputers and modems can make local phone calls to these regional libraries, or dial an 800 number to the central state library to gain access to the system for online catalog searching and electronic mail for requesting inter-library loan materials. The four state college campus libraries use existing microwave links for access to the computer center in Waterbury. Norwich University is connected via a dedicated line to its affiliate Vermont College. Decnet circuits over leased phone lines link the Vaxs at Middlebury, the State College, and the Norwich University computer centers to a router at DOL in Montpelier. Multiplexors on a leased phone line link the DOL computer and UVM systems; all Decnet nodes have access to the DOL-UVM ports. With recent changes in telephone company data service tariffs, costs for the leased lines have been reduced by approximately 50%, so that total costs for library linkage in the state are approximately $3000 per month. The most significant start-up charges for the network development were purchase of the router and modems to link the DRA nodes on the network; other telecommunications hardware was already in place or purchased for each institution's individual implementation of an automated library system. Recent costs in upgrading some communications hardware have been offset by reduced phone line charges.

Preliminary investigation, based on interviews with library staff and on analysis of system accounting logs, indicates that network usage is highly variable, with significant differences among academic and public libraries' and their patrons' uses of the system. The two principal uses of the network are online catalog searching and interlibrary loan mail messaging. Users at the state library and at public libraries who access the system typically are staff; users at the academic sites on the network comprise both end users (students and faculty) as well as library staff.

Evaluation of actual network usage is difficult because not every individual type of transaction is logged to the system. This study utilizes standard system reports of network usernames and connection times for analysis. Several trends are apparent [detailed analyses are not included in this published summary, but will be presented and are available from the author]. A majority of the network connections made on a daily basis are in support of ILL processing; these connections principally are initiated by the DOL regional libraries and State College campuses, but involve system wide mail processing on all nodes. Staff and patrons at Middlebury primarily use the system as a link for searching the UVM catalog; only rarely are other library catalogs searched. In contrast, when searching remote catalogs, public access catalog users at the State College libraries search Middlebury or UVM on a more equal basis. Public and school libraries that access the system via DOL principally search the state library holdings in anticipation of placing ILL requests; half of these smaller libraries also search the catalogs of the larger, networked academic institutions at least once a month, and a few dozen of the smaller libraries search the larger libraries two to three times a week.

In addition to public service functions, the network is also used to support some cataloging activities. Catalogers at the State Colleges check the other sites' catalogs to verify headings. Staff at a few public libraries check the networked libraries for more difficult-to-catalog titles, and one of the larger public libraries in the state regularly uses the network for a retrospective conversion project.

The network is not used for cooperative collection development, but does support other types of resource sharing. For example, the State Library maintains a file of current Vermont legislation and supreme court decisions, accessible to all libraries on the network.

Although difficult to quantify in all cases, significant value has been added to library services as a result of the network. Users benefit from decreased interlibrary loan turnaround time among institutions in the state, which has been cut by approximately one-third. The interlibrary loan process itself has changed, with the network providing users with more sources for loans (higher recall), and greater control over the actual materials requested, with knowledge at the time the loan is requested that an item is available (higher precision). In some instances, public libraries that previously borrowed only a few dozen books a year are now borrowing more than two hundred books for their patrons; interlibrary loan traffic among the state college campuses has increased, as well as traffic from UVM to fulfill Middlebury requests. Staffing responsibilities have shifted in many libraries to accommodate changes in ILL, but no new staff additions have been required.

Public services in all libraries have benefitted by having other catalogs available as a research and verification tool. Reference staff have the added value of colleagues' advice and suggestions available via electronic mail queries and responses (used among the State Colleges, and public libraries and DOL).

Direct cost savings were achieved at Middlebury, through use of dial-out modems over the network node at DOL to local Tymnet and Telenet (previously Middlebury had to dial long distance to reach these carriers). Cataloging costs for authority control verification at the State Colleges and for retrospective conversion at public libraries have been contained as a result of the network.

Future enhancements to VALS will offer additional value to library services in Vermont. Using the existing telecommunications network, new services will include access to local data files, such as Vermont newspaper indexes. This project, using data compiled by staff at Middlebury and UVM on PCs, will be made available on the DOL system to all network and dialin users, without any modification of the network (the indexing software has been purchased by the state library). Members of VALS are actively evaluating the local mounting of journal indexes; sharing the costs of license fees and disk storage may make this information resource more readily affordable to Vermont libraries. Expanded access to remote library catalogs on the Internet is being explored by way of VAL3 logons to the Middlebury system. Looking further into the future, NOTIS and Data Research are each involved in projects for Open Systems Interconnection; as the principle library vendors in the state, future implementation of OSI will lead to a new network environment, for which costs cannot at this point be predicted, but one that Vermont should be well positioned to take advantage of. As decisions are made to make enhanced information services available, network traffic will increase and may necessitate upgraded circuits and equipment to support higher bandwidth in the future. In light of shrinking financial resources, new sources for funding may be required to enable Vermont libraries to take advantage of information resources and technologies when the present network reaches its capacity. Cooperative analysis and planning among the libraries continues, as we determine the most beneficial information services for the many different types of libraries that comprise the Vermont Automated Library System.

UNIX ON THE LIBRARY SCENE

Kathleen Robertson, University of Hawaii at Manoa

Keywords: UNIX, library software

Abstract: UNIX has, in the recent past, been best know as an operating system for scientific workstations such as Suns. It is installed in many academic settings and is praised as being " hardware independent". But as the UNIX operating system becomes more common, the emerging picture is not simple. There are many branches to the UNIX family tree: Ultrix, A/UX and Xenix, to name a few. The various types of UNIX are not interchangeable; recent releases will not automatically run software developed under previous releases. Some UNIX varieties are linked to certain hardware platforms and will not run on other equipment. This session will present an overview of the UNIX family tree and its development. It will present a survey of library application software running under UNIX.

1. UNIX development

In the article, "Automated System Marketplace, 1990," Walton and Bridge note a trend away from turnkey systems toward "software-only" sales and an "open" system environment. UNIX is a major influence in this trend. Although, it's impact is being felt now, UNIX is not really new. The earliest version was written at Bell Laboratories in 1969, by Ken Thompson for an idle DEC PDP-7. Various motives have been ascribed for this initial activity. One is that the Bell Labs patent department needed a patent document preparation tool. This is the reason that UNIX has always excelled at text management, and that text is the accepted medium of communication in the interactive operating system (Christian 1983: 4). A more humorous version attributes the invention of UNIX to Ken Thompson's desire to play a game called Space Travel, which simulated the movements of major celestial bodies in the solar system (Azzara and Boyle, 1990: 3). To use the old PDP-7, he began to write an operating system for it. Rather than write the system in assembly language, which would have made it machine dependent, Thompson wrote a language called B for the system. By 1971, UNIX had been ported to a PDP-11/20 and used by the patent office. In 1973, Dennis Ritchie developed the C language and rewrote the UNIX operating system in it. The name UNIX is a pun on Multics, a major main frame operating system when UNIX was first being written.

UNIX begin to spread within the Bell organization. AT&T, Bell's parent firm, was a communications company, not a computer firm, and therefor, was not permitted to sell UNIX commercially. Starting in 1975, universities and research facilities were allowed to acquire the UNIX license and source code at a very low fee. This made a great contribution to its spread. In source code form, UNIX was much easier to change and customize. University of California, Berkeley became a major force in UNIX development. The Defense Advanced Research Projects Agency (DARPA) funded the Berkeley team to develop a network communications protocol. This project lead to ARPANET and its descendant, Internet. It also lead to the Berkeley Software Distribution releases of UNIX, 3BSD and 4BSD, and later versions (Leffler et al. 1989: 11). The Berkeley releases enabled UNIX to run on large machines.

2. UNIX today

UNIX evolution has continued on many fronts. AT&T and Berkeley have continued to put out new releases. Other developers have put out commercial versions, such as Microsoft XENIX for microcomputers. User groups have greatly influenced UNIX development by writing and distributing utilities and software. There are also "UNIX-like" systems that have been developed outside the AT&T-Berkeley axis. There are no universally accepted standards covering what utilities (capabilities) a UNIX system should contain. If a system is "unbundled" it could lack some routines needed to support certain software packages (Clukey 1985: 20). When a UNIX version is considered for purchase, which utilities are included should be clarified. When a software package is considered, it's vital to identify which version of the system it requires for support. With a UNIX "look alike" system, it is important to check that it includes all utilities (functions) the software package needs.

UNIX is composed of the core operating system, an extensive library of utilities and a flexible shell programming level. Most variants can support multi-user operations and multi-tasking. It can support a network linking many types of hardware and peripherals. UNIX is appearing in more offices and libraries. One of its most vaulted attributes is its portability. However, this should not be interpreted to mean equivalency. Unix varieties are each unique and linked to specific computers, called platforms. Software running under UNIX for a Hewlett-Packard (HP) cannot be transferred directly to a Sun workstation. A program written for one release of the operating system will not necessarily run on a different release. So questions of hardware and software compatibility have not been eliminated. But, in the UNIX open system environment, there is a greater likelihood that a software package can be adapted, rather than replaced, if there is an equipment change. When selecting UNIX based packages, the release and hardware configuration must be identified.

There are several large database management systems (DBMS) available for UNIX. Informix, Ingres, Oracle, ACCELL and Sybase are the main commercial offerings (Rogers 1990). Ingres is the basis of the Carlyle product. Custom programming could render other DBMS appropriate for library applications. Eric LeBlanc, at the Dominion Astrophysical Observatory Library in Victoria, B.C., has been faced with hardware and system changes from VMS to UNIX. He is developing routines in Sybase to support his library applications.

3. **UNIX in the Library**

The following is a partial list of vendors offering library/information handling products that run under UNIX and UNIX-like systems.

3.1 AT&T Bell Laboratories
In a 1988 article, Robert K. Waldstein described SLIMMER, an acronym for Special Library Information Module - Multiple Environment Retrieval. This package was developed by Bell Labs to meet the needs of their Library Network. While not available commercially, this article gives a tantalizing picture of a highly elaborated system.

3.2 Carlyle Systems, Inc.
Carlyle has cataloguing, online and circulation modules running on Sun workstations. These are available as turnkey packages or in a software-only version. A DEC Ultrix version is currently under development.

3.3 Centel Federal Services Corporation
DataLib is a modularized library management system including records management and litigation support. It runs under UNIX V on ICL, AT&T and HP platforms.

3.4 CLSI
CLSI markets their package on Sequent equipment as a turnkey offering. The company has plans to explore porting their software to other hardware platforms in the near future.

3.5 Comstow Information Services
Comstow, the producer of the well known Bibliotech Library Software, announced the release of its UNIX offering in February of this year. Named Bibliotix, this package utilizes Empress, a relational database management system and fourth generation language. It will run on HP/Apollo workstations and the Sun SPARCstations. Bibliotix includes a cataloging/indexing module, a retrieval module and authority control.

3.6 Cuadra Associates, Inc.
Cuadra's STAR was once linked to a single hardware platform. Now, it runs on several, including the Sun Series 3 and SPARCstations. Written in C, STAR is a multi-user DBMS.

3.7 Data Trek, Inc.
Data Trek offers its software for a variety of hardware from microcomputers to VAX mainframes. Having acquired a UNIX compiler, Data Trek is now prepared to develop a version of the package for the hardware platform of the customer's choice.

3.8 Dynix, Inc.
This major player in the library software arena produces packages that run on HP platforms.

3.9 Information Dimensions
A subsidiary of the Batelle Development Corporation, this firm offers TECHLIBplus, a modularized information management system built on the strength of the BASIS search application (now enhanced and called BASISplus). TECHLIBplus runs on HP platforms and supports VT100, VT200, VT300 terminals and compatibles.

3.10 Innovative Interfaces, Inc.
INNOPAC (online catalogue) and INNOVACQ (technical services), on Convergent Technologies and MIPS computers, are among the turnkey products offered by this quickly growing firm. They also have a software-only version available for DEC equipment.

3.11 Ringgold Management Systems, Inc.
This firm offers both UNIX System V.3 and XENIX based products.

3.12 Sirsi Corporation
Unicorn, this firm's fully integrated set of library management modules, is written in C. Versions are available for a range of equipment from micros to large mainframes.

3.13 Sobeco/MultiLIS
This Canadian vendor offers a package running under UNIX 5, release 2. Most of its installations are in Canada and the East Coast.

3.14 Unsis
PALS, this company's best known library product, does not run under UNIX. Unsis is currently working with third party developers on UNIX based offerings.

4. **REFERENCES**

Azzara, M., Boyle, B. 1990
    UNIX's last 20 years examined. *UNIX Solutions*, August, 3,5.

Christian, Kaare. 1983
    The Unix Operating System. New York: John Wiley & Sons.

Clukey, L.P. 1985
    UNIX & XENIX Demystified. Blue Ridge Summit, PA: Tab Books Inc.

Leffler, S.J., et al. 1989
    The Design and Implementation of 4.3BSD UNIX Operating System. New York: Addison-Wesley.

Rodgers, Ulka. 1990
    UNIX Database Management Systems. New York: Prentice-Hall.

Waldstein, R.K. 1988.
    SLIMMER—A UNIX System-Based Information Retrieval System. *Reference Services Review* 16 (1-2): 69-76.

Walton, R.A., Bridge, F.R. 1990
    Automated System Marketplace 1990, *Library Journal*, April 1, 1990, 55-66. This annual survey of the field is an excellent source of up-to-date vendor address information.

LET'S MAKE A DEAL: DONOR-DRIVEN LIBRARY SYSTEMS IN A NON-PROFIT INSTITUTION

Carol J. Snyder, Snyder Associates

Keywords: Donations, Library Systems, Non-Profits

Abstract: This paper will focus on the role of donations in the automation of a non-profit institution's library. It discusses the advantages and disadvantages of accepting hardware and software donations and offers warnings on the pitfalls of mixing and matching mini-based and microcomputer equipment without adequate training, maintenance, and technical support.

1. BACKGROUND

A new position was created as Electronic Media Coordinator in a non-profit institution's library. The purpose was to create an electronic library to support one of the missions of the institution to stimulate interest in and further public understanding of technology. A five year plan was established to add electronic media and to automate the library with as little money as possible. This project would enable 1,000 patrons of the library, including 400 staff, volunteers, and Massachusetts teachers, to enjoy access to current information. In addition, approximately 1.8 million visitors a year could see technology in action.

2. LIST OF DONATIONS FOR A LOCAL AREA NETWORK

Donations valuing over $75,000 from two major computer companies enabled library automation to commence. The library received the following:
1) a 80386 super microcomputer which was UNIX-based and contained a DOS partition (mini-based system)
2) 10 dumb terminals
3) 2 laser printers
4) 2 modems
5) 1 tape drive
6) operating system software
7) a 80386 DOS microcomputer and internal modem

A third donation came from another department within the institution and consisted of 6 nine year old 8088 pcs.

3. ADVANTAGES OF DONATIONS FOR THE LIBRARY

   Advantages for the library were these: 1) immediate implementation of library automation and 2) provision for state-of-the-art equipment which otherwise would have been beyond the means of the institution's capital budget.

4. ADVANTAGES FOR THE DONOR

   Advantages for the donors were 1) a tax write off and 2) good public relations in service to the community.

5. CONSEQUENCES OF ACCEPTING DONATIONS

   It was later discovered that the donations did not provide adequate memory, processing speed, or storage for all of the library's functions. The application was very DOS intensive and did not mesh well in the UNIX environment. Hence, the equipment did not meet the library's needs 100%. The library also required more equipment, technical support, maintenance, and training than was donated in order to complete the project.

5.1 MORE DISADVANTAGES OF DONATIONS

   Disadvantages occurred over the length of the project:
   1) equipment not 100% suited to the library environment
   2) immediate outlay of money still needed for "incidentals" to piece the two donations together
   3) ongoing budget for technical support, maintenance, and training not available
   4) donor's time frame for installation and support slowed progress of the project
   5) almost total dependency upon the computer company for continuing support
   6) extra time required to satisfy donor's desires for marketing and open houses,
   7) extra staff needed to get the system "up and running" immediately to show progress to administrators

6. WHAT REALLY HAPPENED

   The Massachusetts economy turned on the computer companies. A buyout and reorganization of one of the major donors occurred. Turnover of staff on both sides left no written, legal agreement. Thus, the library was never officially registered as an owner. There was no telephone technical support, no maintenance contract, and no training for the first donation.

   The second donation had no continuing maintenance contract, and no institution funds appeared for technical support, maintenance, or training.

   Likewise, the third donation of obsolescent technology had no budget to upgrade or maintain the machines.

   Budget woes descended upon the non-profit institution, and the library had an almost non-existent automation budget. Furthermore, budget cuts necessitated termination of 26 positions, including that of Electronic Media Coordinator.

6. CRUCIAL TIP

Is a donation the way to proceed? There is "no such thing as a free lunch!"

6.1 CRUCIAL TIPS--EXPERTS

What the Information Specialist encountered was "experts" who were not expert in everything. The library vendor did not know the computer manufacturer's hardware. The donor's engineers did not know the software application in the library environment. Technology changes so rapidly that no one can keep totally up-to-date.

The crucial tip is this: You can not rely on any outside experts to do your job for you. They never know your environment and the pieces making up that environment as well as you do. Trust yourself! It is up to you, the systems manager, to investigate things thoroughly before jumping into the frying pan.

7. WARNINGS ON MIXING & MATCHING DONATIONS OF MINI-BASED AND MICROCOMPUTER EQUIPMENT IN A LOCAL AREA NETWORK

Based upon my experience, do not mix and match technical innovations, which require much support, with donations, which tend to receive little support.

If you decide to go for donations, aim for donations that you know will work on a stand alone basis. Make sure that there is adequate technical support, maintenance, training, and an ongoing budget! In the long run, it costs more money to mix and match than to buy an existing, proven system. You will spend countless hours in planning, inventing, trying to mesh the pieces, and "making do" with what you have.

BEYOND THE ONLINE CATALOG: CURRENT DEVELOPMENTS AND FUTURE DIRECTIONS OF NEW ENGLAND LIBRARY AUTOMATION

Diane R. Tebbetts, University of New Hampshire

Abstract: This 1990 study surveys the development of automated integrated systems in nine Association of Research Libraries (ARL) in New England. It provides a five year update on earlier research and allows comparison of results between 1985 and 1990. Analysis of the survey responses indicates that although these libraries are still working to fully implement their online systems, they also are developing strategies to expand the online catalog. These strategies include: 1) enriching the online catalog, 2) connecting to networks, and 3) developing user-friendly software. These trends are leading to other developments in libraries, such as: 1) relying on local expertise, 2) buying standard hardware, 3) developing flexible software, 4) linking disparate systems, and 5) planning for the next system.
    These nine research libraries in New England serve as a microcosm of library automation in the United States. Their experiences mirror those of other libraries across the country, and provide us with an understanding of the current developments and a glimpse of the future directions in library automation.

1. INTRODUCTION

    This 1990 study surveys the development of automated integrated systems in nine Association of Research Libraries (ARL) in New England. It provides a five year update on earlier research and allows comparison of results between 1985 and 1990.
    In 1985, emphasis in these libraries was being placed on acquiring and implementing online integrated systems. Six of the nine libraries had purchased or were in the process of purchasing integrated online library systems. In the years between 1985 and 1990, many of these libraries have continued toward this goal. However, due to vendor instability, they have had to change systems or add modules from other systems. Analysis of the survey responses indicates that although these libraries are still working to fully implement their online systems, they are also developing strategies to expand the online catalog. These strategies include: enriching the online catalog by adding externally-developed records and databases, by developing local databases and by linking different databases; connecting to campus, consortial, regional, and national networks; and developing user-friendly software by enhancing workstation design and by designing user-friendly interfaces. To accomplish these new developments, libraries have had to develop local expertise, to buy standard hardware, to emphasize flexible software, to link disparate systems, and to plan for the next system. These results not only indicate a trend in New England ARL libraries but also mirror developments across the country.

2. RESEARCH METHODOLOGY

    In 1985, an extensive study of these nine libraries was conducted employing the case study method (Ref. 1). Individual interviews of the directors and systems librarians resulted in a detailed analysis of the libraries and their automation efforts. In 1990, a follow-up telephone survey was conducted to determine developments in the intervening years. The Director and/or Systems Librarian of each library was interviewed using the open-ended interview technique which allows the respondents to answer in their own words and expand on their responses.

Some of the issues probed were:
- Whether the library was implementing the same system as in 1985
- What changes have been made and why
- How new developments in networking were affecting them
- What changes were taking place within the library and on the campus as a result of new technology
- What were the factors influencing decision-making in automation
- What was the anticipated future direction of library automation.

3. STUDY RESULTS

This study revealed several new developments in library automation. Although these libraries are still emphasizing the automation of the card catalog and internal library operations, there is a clear movement towards the expansion of resources. In 1985, all of the libraries were concentrating on retrospective conversion of their collections; automating serials control, acquisitions, and circulation; and introducing the online catalog. In 1990, these are still important considerations, but new concerns have been added. The ability to connect to networks of all kinds is essential; the capacity to add new databases — locally-created or externally-developed — is highly desirable; flexibility to connect disparate systems is crucial; ease of access by end-users is fundamental; and local expertise to handle the systems is vital.

In 1985, the library directors were tending to opt for turnkey systems. In this type of system the vendors supplied everything — hardware, software, system development, maintenance and support. With the vendor instability in this volatile market, however, this option proved to be very risky. Libraries found themselves having to switch systems and add on new subsystems. This, combined with the new networking and database developments, has led library directors to develop and to rely on local expertise — both in the library and on campus.

Thus, five years has seen a dramatic change in the direction and implementation of library automation in the ARL Libraries in New England.

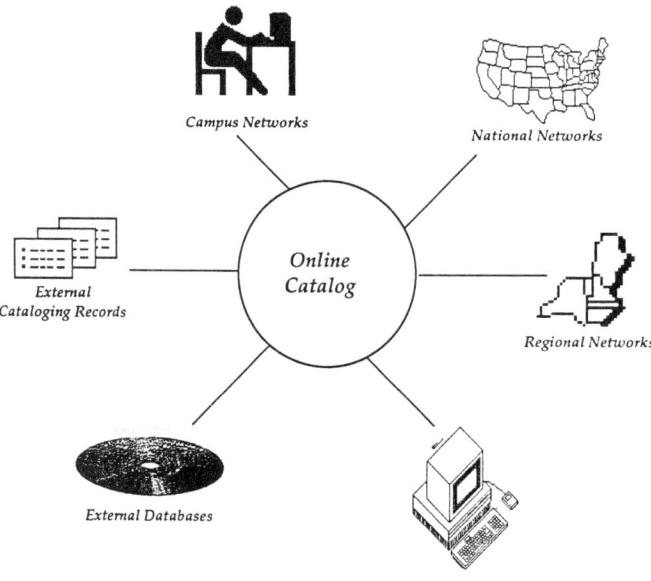

Figure 1: Expanding the Online Catalog

4. CURRENT DEVELOPMENTS AND FUTURE DIRECTIONS OF LIBRARY AUTOMATION

From the results of this survey, it is clear that libraries are moving to expand the resources of their collections by adding more access to their materials and by adding new databases to their systems. Their strategies include the following developments.

4.1 Enriching the Online Catalog

Adding externally-developed cataloging records

The libraries that are the furthest along in their development have turned their attention to developing their online systems more fully. They are doing this by adding records from sources other than the libraries' cataloging departments. One systems librarian estimates that only half of the records on his system has been input by catalogers. The data are coming from a variety of sources. Other library personnel are putting in some of the records — circulation staff and acquisitions staff. Some of the records are coming from external sources. One library is loading data from the Center for Research Libraries, as well as a regional union list and major microform records. Another library has a shared database with several libraries contributing records to the system. A third library plans to add U.S. Government Printing Office tapes to provide access to government documents. It is becoming essential to be able to add records from a variety of sources, but the libraries have to maintain control over what is added to the system. In one library, the Systems Office provides this control whereas reorganized technical services departments provide the necessary supervision of the database in three other libraries. In one of these libraries the unit is called the Bibliographic Control Unit while another library is applying the team concept in which teams are responsible for handling particular types or categories of material. In the third library, a database librarian position has been created with emphasis on how the database looks. Another library has changed to a catalog maintenance unit and another is implementing post-cataloging authority control. Certainly, the addition of records from several sources is having a major impact on the composition and control of the online catalog.

Adding externally-developed databases

In addition to adding external records to the online catalog, libraries are expanding their resources by adding additional databases. Many of these databases are indexes to periodical literature. For example, two libraries have loaded Medline (the online version of Index Medicus) and one has added Current Contents from the Institute for Scientific Information.
As well as indexes to periodicals, some full-text databases are being added to the online catalog. One library has added a full-text encyclopedia and Shakespeare's plays. This library is also looking at additional databases but copyright considerations and vendor reluctance to sell or lease tapes are slowing down the process (Ref. 2).
Other libraries are interested in loading tapes but hardware restrictions and software incompatibility is making it difficult for them to do so. One library predicts it will be adding external databases within a year. Another library is looking at a new system that will make full-text searching possible, and two other libraries have similar plans as they move to new online systems.
Therefore, this is certainly a major issue in most of these libraries. Some are currently adding databases while others plan to do so in the near future.
Many of the libraries that are not yet adding tapes to their online system are providing access to external databases on CD-ROM. All of the libraries have CD-ROM indexes and three are working on networking the CD's. One has its CD indexes on a LAN but not on the campus network, while another is planning on using CD's for its online catalog. However, two systems librarians and one director view CD's as a temporary technology and tape loading as the future direction for providing access to external databases.

Developing local databases

As well as providing externally-developed databases, these libraries are producing and maintaining databases of local interest. These databases cover a wide range of materials. One library has a guide to the library online and is looking at other campus information; another has a sheet music collection and an index to the state's newspapers. Another library is exploring the possibility of adding databases through a consortium computer.

The libraries exploring local database development are those that have their card catalogs almost completely online. Once the library has its collection completely accessible, the next step is to provide additional resources. Of course, the hardware must be large enough to accommodate these additional databases and the software must be flexible so that systems librarians and catalogers can manipulate the data.

Although none of these libraries have imaging or voice capabilities yet, many see these as future developments. One systems librarian projects imaging of the library's manuscript materials as a future development.

Although the development of local databases is only in the beginning stages for these libraries, it certainly appears to be an important trend for the future.

Linking different systems

It is becoming crucial for these libraries to be able to link disparate systems. At the present time, several of these libraries have had to add modules from different systems, and they are finding it very difficult to link them, especially if the main system runs on proprietary hardware. Two of these libraries are looking at new software that will run on a large IBM mainframe while another has opted for software that runs on a DEC computer. Still another library has selected new software that is UNIX- based. All of these libraries are moving away from proprietary hardware and software, because it is extremely difficult to add databases or link systems not on standard equipment.

4.2 Connecting to Networks

Accessing campus networks

Once the library's catalog becomes available online, the next step is to provide remote access. Professors want to be able to dial-in from their offices, and students want access from their dormitory rooms. Therefore, the ability to connect to the campus network becomes essential. All but one of the academic libraries surveyed are connected to the campus network, although they are in varying stages of availability. One library has 6,000 terminals connected to the system with the capability of accommodating 60-65 simultaneous users. Another library logged 16,000 dial-in sessions last year, while a third has 425-430 dedicated terminals, two dozen networked ports and two dozen dial-in ports. Still another has a microwave link to a branch campus as well as access to the campus network. Clearly, this is a major development for these libraries and the library's hardware and software must be compatible with the campus system.

Connecting to national networks

The latest development in library networking is the ability to connect to the national networks, especially the Internet, an interlocking system of regional networks. Libraries are making their online catalogs available on this network, as well as gaining access to other resources. All but two of the academic libraries have access to the Internet, and half of these have their online catalogs available on the network. The other half plan to make them available soon depending on the ability of their systems to interface with the network.

Therefore, it is becoming essential for libraries to have the capability to connect to national networks. Many types of resources are becoming available on these networks in addition to individual library catalogs. For instance, OCLC is making some of its services available over the Internet. It is becoming evident that this is an important trend for the future.

Linking with systems in a consortial arrangement

In addition to campus networks and national networks, some of these libraries want to be able to connect with libraries in other arrangements. For instance, one library in a consortium of closely-related libraries wants to develop special software for accessing these systems. Another library wants to be able to link with libraries having the same system and is working to develop this interface. The ARL public library is providing a centralized database for several smaller public libraries in the region. Still another library is involved in a statewide public access catalog project. These projects add another dimension to an already complicated picture of interlocking networks.

However, it is certainly evident that networking is a fast-moving development in the library automation field, and it is essential for libraries to be able to connect to a variety of networks from local to regional to national. Planning for this capability is an essential ingredient in the library automation effort.

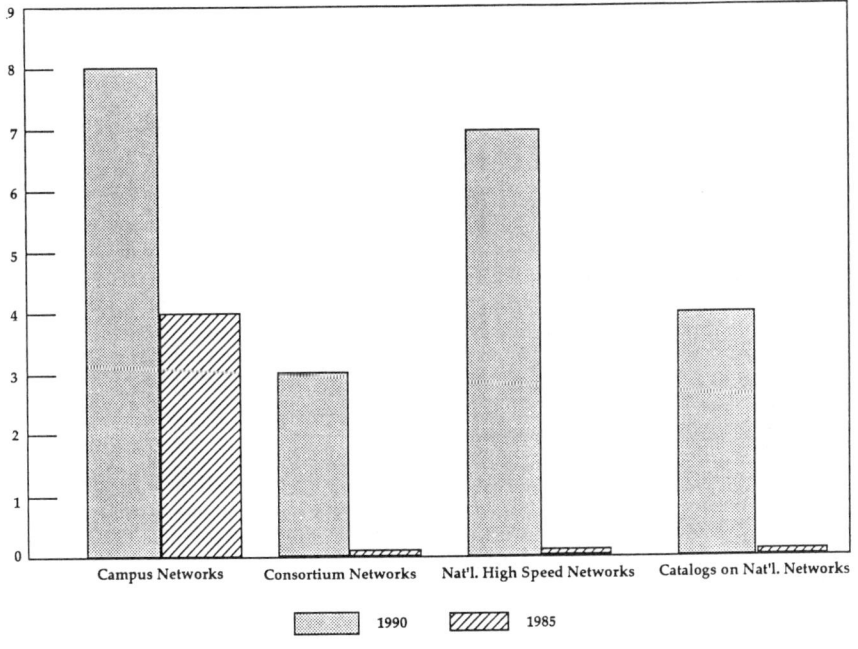

Figure 2: Libraries Connected to Networks

4.3 Developing User-friendly Software

Enhancing workstation design

With the enrichment of the online catalog by adding records and databases and linking disparate systems as well as networking to external sources, it is becoming essential to provide the user with help in using these systems. To remember different commands and protocols for each system is almost impossible. Therefore, the libraries must work on user-friendly software to make the systems easier to use.

Some of the libraries are concentrating their efforts on workstation design. One library is involved in a comprehensive effort to develop the user interface based on Macintosh features and conventions (Ref. 3). Another library is emphasizing workstations as "windows on the Library" while a third is seeing more focus on client-server architecture.

Designing user-friendly interfaces

While some libraries are concentrating on workstation design, other libraries are working to develop user-friendly software on the mainframe computers. One library is working with other libraries and the hardware manufacturer to develop a software package that greatly simplifies access to the system. Still another library's system analyst envisions a centralized computer with a shell script that would log a user on to a particular library's system; thus, alleviating the necessity of the user knowing a particular system.

From this study it appears that user-friendly software is developing in two directions — one microcomputer based, the other mainframe connected. Whichever trend takes precedence, it is clear that developing software to help users through the maze of systems and resources is becoming not just helpful but a necessity.

5. ADDITIONAL STUDY RESULTS

Based on the trends outlined above, as well as other factors such as vendor instability, these libraries are making decisions that differ markedly from those being made in 1985. In 1990, these libraries seem to be following these directions.

5.1 Relying on Local Expertise

With the volatility in the vendor marketplace, libraries can no longer rely on the expertise of the vendor's programmers and computer specialists to supply enhancements to the system. In addition, the need to enrich the online catalog by adding external records and databases requires locally-based programmers. The need to connect with campus, regional, and national networks also requires local computer experience. Thus, libraries are increasing their capability in this area.

Expanding library systems departments

In this survey, library systems departments have shown the most dramatic change in the library's organizational structure. All of the academic libraries have seen an increase in systems personnel. The average size of a systems office is four persons with a director, programmer, operator, and documentation specialist. However, some of the libraries have much larger staffs. In all of the systems offices there is an emphasis on service. One library, in particular, completely reorganized the systems office to make it a real service unit with first line support for the online system. Another systems office has increased by 300%. Some positions responsible for the database are located in technical services departments. One library has a database librarian while another has a bibliographic control unit. The ARL public library has a large systems staff and needs more. Thus, it is evident that libraries are increasing their systems staffs to handle the expanded online catalog and its related hardware and software.

Cooperating with campus computer services

In addition to increasing systems staffs within the library, the academic libraries are forging closer relationships with their campus computer services. One library has had a long-term relationship with the campus computer office. In this arrangement, the library systems office is responsible for automation development and programming while the college computer services is in charge of facilities management, installation and operator coverage. At another campus, the responsibility is split between library systems and campus computer services with front-line support of the system in the library. On other campuses, the campus computer office serves in an advisory capacity. This is becoming essential, especially with the arrival of the networking issues.

Therefore, it is becoming absolutely necessary for libraries to develop their local computer expertise and to establish close ties with campus computer services, so they can take advantage of additional resources and provide the best possible system for their faculties and students.

5.2 Buying Standard Hardware

The 1990 survey indicated a dramatic shift to standard hardware. In 1985, many of these libraries had purchased or were in the process of buying proprietary systems which consisted of a hardware-software package. However, in 1990, these libraries were switching to the large computer companies such as IBM and DEC — five had or were looking at IBM, two were on DEC, one on DG, and one on a UNIX-based system. One reason for this change is, of course, the vendor instability. Other reasons involve the new developments. Adding external records and databases requires more memory and the large mainframes provide the necessary space. In addition, it is usually easier to interface these disparate systems on standard hardware. Networking also is much easier when using standard hardware. Thus, the new trends in online catalog development are pushing libraries in the direction of purchasing standard hardware with a lot of memory.

5.3 Developing Flexible Software

In addition to buying standard hardware, libraries are trying to find flexible software which will allow them to interface systems and connect to different computers and networks. One library purchased a system that would run on any UNIX-based equipment. Another library is in discussions with a software vendor to produce a system for a large IBM mainframe. Another library has bought a system that will run on DEC or IBM. Thus, the trends in software purchasing is to buy that which offers the most flexibility. Those libraries with extremely large collections usually opt for the IBM-based systems which will run on large mainframes, whereas smaller institutions sometimes choose software that will run on any UNIX-based equipment. Whatever the choice, flexibility is certainly an important consideration.

5.4 Linking Disparate Systems

As has been discussed, the ability to link systems is becoming vital. Vendor instability has made it necessary for libraries to purchase subsystems from other vendors because the original system has not been fully developed. It then becomes very important to link these systems, but often it is very difficult to do so. One library has built its system with different modules. It has chosen what it considers to be the best module for each function — acquisitions, serials control, circulation, etc. — and then interfaced them. Another library is following this procedure with a focus on a distributed model of library services. It has selected a CD-system for its online catalog and will choose individual modules for its other functions. Still another library has had to add acquisitions and circulation modules from one system to an online catalog by another vendor. The other libraries are still following the route of the integrated system but only one has a fully integrated system at this time. Even with the integrated systems, these libraries are finding that they want to link to other systems and networks. Therefore, it is becoming an extremely important issue in library automation.

5.5 Planning for the Next System

The results of this survey, combined with the earlier 1985 research, have made it clear that librarians must be planning for automation on a continuous basis. New developments such as networking, combined with the availability of new resources, make it imperative for librarians to consider new or upgraded hardware and software. One director in this survey stated that automation is a continuous process, while the Associate Director of another library indicated she was purchasing one system but already planning for the next system.

Library automation is a fast-moving, dynamic process as is computerization in general. Librarians must be flexible and willing to change to take advantage of the latest developments. They must plan for the future realizing that new and/or upgraded systems are inevitable. Therefore, they must build their current systems with as much flexibility as possible, and always be thinking of the future.

6.   CONCLUSION

This study has revealed that libraries are moving to expand and enrich their online catalogs by adding external records to increase access to their holdings. In addition, they are adding externally-developed databases to add access to periodical literature, government documents, and full-text materials such as encyclopedias, dictionaries, and literary works. Some libraries are creating their own indexes or putting local manuscript materials online. Providing access to materials off campus via regional and national networks is also becoming extremely important.

With all these developments libraries are finding they need more systems expertise both in the library and on campus. They are also learning that they need to buy large, standard equipment and flexible software. Finally, library managers are coming to realize that library automation is a continuous process and they must constantly be planning for the future and the next system.

Libraries must be dynamic systems that are ready to adapt to new circumstances and take advantage of new developments because library automation is a fast-moving, changing environment.

7.   REFERENCES

1. Tebbetts, Diane R., *Integrating Microcomputers in ARL Libraries: Management Considerations*. Field Research Project Report for the Doctor of Arts Degree. Boston, MA: Graduate School of Library & Information Science, Simmons College, 1985.

2. Klemperer, Katharine, "New Dimensions for the Online Catalog: The Dartmouth College Library Experience." *Information Technology and Libraries* 8 (2), 138-45, 1989.

3. *Dartmouth College Information System*. Hanover, N.H.: Dartmouth College, 1990.

THE POWER OF LIBRARY ADMINISTRATORS MEETS THE POWER OF TECHNOLOGY

Kieth C. Wright, University of North Carolina, Greensboro

Keywords: Resistance to change, Management of change, Staff development, Planning

Abstract: Integrated computer-based library systems have the capacity to create lots of management information for the library administrator. The systems are upon us; the question remains can administrators use the power of these systems to empower their libraries? Or, will these new systems simply create more demands on administrators, technical and public services staff and users -- thereby weakening the entire library service system?

    The major reason for considering computer applications in libraries is increased efficiency in information management and communications. Workstations allow the administrator to find information, process information and disseminate information much more efficiently. When one workstation is tied to other workstations through a local area network that information management and communications process becomes even more efficient. Text and numeric data which once had to be assembled by hand can now be accessed using integrated word processing programs. Analysis of operating efficiency of the local library or library OPAC system can be done at the workstation using spreadsheet programs. Many repetitive tasks can be handled with minimum effort. Information from remote sites can be acquired easily through online database services. Higher quality printed and graphics materials can be produced. The library administrator can even change what the library does as well as how it is done.

    Effective library information management is possible. However there are a number of obstacles to creating library-based systems which will work. The major obstacle is resistance to change and the inability of administrators to overcome that resistance. This paper focuses on techniques for managing change in the library.

1. INTRODUCTION: SETTING THE TECHNOLOGICAL STAGE

Andriole sets the power of computer technologies in this context (Ref. 1):

People are more expensive than technology. In the past,
data processing hardware cost millions of dollars and
required huge investments of money, space and facilities.

Now, microcomputers are available at a fraction of the cost of one year of personnel time and are small enough to sit on an individual desk. Customized software can cost many times the price of the machine.

The new technology is increasingly user-friendly. Data processing specialists are less necessary than they were in the past for retrieving and analyzing information. More and more users will interface directly with their own data.

Andriole stresses the economic and human revolution which technology brings into our communities, our homes, and our libraries. This revolution could increase library administrators' power to manage information more effectively in the "information age" and to be a more powerful player in that age. But what about the reality? This paper addresses the process of helping library staff through the change process necessary for the use computer-based technology in our libraries.

2. DEFINING THE IMPACT OF TECHNOLOGY ON LIBRARY ADMINISTRATION

Computer and communications technology are rapidly altering the society in which libraries and library systems operate. More and more information about business and services is available via computer. Steward Brand, in his The Media Lab, states that our ability to digitize information of all types is as important as the invention of the movable type printing press (Ref. 2). The ability to communicate and transform information into a variety of formats make all information more flexible. A much wider variety of information is produced and it tends to remain modifiable over time.

Debuse identifies six technological developments accelerating social change and altering power relationships (Ref. 3): 1) Powerful and portable computers available in home, car, and office, 2) User interface software with graphic interfaces and simple pointing devices (the mouse), 3) Optical storage devices storing up to 550 megabytes of data, 4) Hypermedia to organize and provide access to very large databases by creating and representing multiple levels and relations among parts (or concepts) of a database, 5) Artificial intelligence to perform complex functions using expert systems to assist people finding what they want, 6) Authoring systems which permit the publication and use of hypermedia materials and other interactive publications or programs. He sees these six technologies creating a monumental shift in the ways we share data, create information, and change it dynamically.

Communication by computer is not the same as face-to-face communication. Social structures of society and libraries are affected by these differences. There is less filtering of information in organizations. Business managers now have access to salespersons and customers without the filtering of information through middle management. Customers' complaints, actual sales records, delays in delivery, and cost overruns can no longer be hidden or delayed. Wright's law which states, "negative information does not flow uphill because that's where to money comes from" can be overcome.

The worker with a computer can have access to sales figures, projections, and working documents (unless they are "secured" in the system). Interpretations of "how things are going" are widely spread throughout the system. Such open systems are effective in horizontal organizations which require information and input from a variety of sources. Traditional hierarchical organizations (like libraries) are not so accepting of open access to information throughout the system.

3. THE POWER OF LIBRARY ADMINISTRATORS MEETS THE POWER OF TECHNOLOGY

The question is not, "Will we use these technologies?" but rather, "How will we use these technologies to have the power to meet our library system's goals and objectives?" Online public access catalog system have the capacity to create lots of management information for the library administrator. The systems are upon us; the question remains can administrators use the power of these systems to empower their libraries? Or, will these new systems simply create more demands on administrators, staff and users -- thereby weakening all personnel and the entire library system?

The major reason for considering computers, workstations, local area networks, or electronic mail in libraries is increased efficiency in information management and communications. Workstations allow the administrator to find information, process information and disseminate information much more efficiently. When one administrator's workstation is tied to other workstations through a local area network that information management and communications process becomes even more efficient. Text and numeric data which once had to be assembled by hand can now be accessed using integrated word processing programs. Analysis of operating efficiency of the local library or library system can be done at the workstation using spreadsheet programs. Many repetitive tasks can be handled with minimum effort. Information from remote sites can be acquired easily through online database services. Higher quality printed and graphics materials can be produced. Properly managed, these resources allow the library administrator not only do what he/she did before; he/she can also do things which were not possible before. The library administrator can even change what the library does as well as how it is done. In other words, the administrator can be effective as well as efficient.

4. RESISTANCE TO EFFECTIVE ADMINISTRATIVE USE OF TECHNOLOGY

<u>Scientific American</u> introduces the special section on "the workstation revolution" with these words (Ref. 4):

> Every year new stories about the emergence of faster, more functional, and, in defiance of generations of economists, cheaper computers appear. And every year come new claims that we are in the midst of a revolution. We are in the midst of a revolution. It is not simply because computers are getting smaller and cheaper. The word revolution implies something more dramatic. The computer revolution is about the fundamental change occurring in the relationship between human beings and computers. The way we work with computers is changing dramatically. In this revolution, the workstation has become the most visible agent of change.

From an administrative perspective, the central issue is management of change. The new technologies are introducing new equipment, new processes and methods, new human relationships, and new work responsibilities. These changes means that almost all aspects of the library's work place may be changed. Computers do jobs previously done by people (adding numbers, producing documents, creating graphics, etc.). Some individuals have developed skills in these areas which are now not only obsolete, but also more expensive than computer produced products. Library staff may wonder if their jobs are going to be lost because the computer now does part of the work. Other staff may feel that they can not learn the new way to do work. One way to insure these feelings is to announce in meetings that technology -- especially workstations and local area networks -- will cut the personnel costs of the library.

Many people view change as unusual rather than as a regular part of life. Indeed, a great deal of effort is put into making things stay the same. The pace of technological change in current society is so rapid that many people feel that the technology is driving the work place, and that the equipment is taking precedence over the people. People tend to view technology as either (1) bad -- because it wastes resources, centralizes control, causes loss of personal freedom and dignity, and increases inequality, consumerism, deskilled jobs and eventual unemployment, or (2) good -- because it causes increased personal freedom, more participation, more leisure time, more knowledge, and improved quality of life.

Figure 1 illustrates some potential responses to change as the individual evaluates the impact of the proposed change on him/herself.

Figure 1.

```
A change is ___\ Individuals evaluate ___\ Individuals
proposed    /  impact on themselves  /   respond
```

Individuals can make the following evaluations and responses:

Evaluation	Response
Destructive	Resist openly
Threatening	Resist covertly
Uncertain	Tolerate
Positive	Support, participate

(Ref. 5)

The evaluation of each individual is dependent on (1) the amount of information he/she has about the change, (2) the extent to which he/she can participate in the decision making process about the change, (3) How much the initiator of the change is trusted, and (4) the individual's past experience with change. Thus, the amount of resistance to change is largely dependent on the climate of the organization.

Library administrators have moved to use technology in their operations but have not always considered the consequences for employees. In speaking about library administrator's move toward technology, Dakshinamorti notes (Ref. 6):

> Library organizations were in such a hurry to be included in this (technological) transformation that few contemplated the resulting effect of computer-aided systems on their employees.

Some libraries are clearly victims of the "get the equipment, then worry about the people" syndrome. Since the introduction of technology into the library will affect working processes at all levels of the library, it is important that all staff be involved in the process of deciding on the uses of technology. The staff should be involved in the discussion of what areas of work the technology will impact, the variety of technological resources which could be utilized, and the process by which the choice of technologies is made.

Librarians and support staff who have worked with computers in the library will be the most likely to accept the new systems and processes necessary to make library workstations and local area networks operate successfully. If this original anxiety can be overcome, many people are willing to learn about these technologies and how to use them.

Even the most willing staff members who have very positive attitudes about computer related technology may be frustrated by the necessity of sitting at a terminal for long periods of time, waiting for the computer, or having something unexpected happen while they are working. People are concerned about costs -- what will this change cost me in time and dollars? People want to know what the impact of the technology system will be on their work routines and their relationships with other workers (and their families). People may also worry that they do not have the ability to learn how to use the system effectively.

Some library staff members have had experience with computers, on-line services, and word processing, and other staff (because of assignment or personal preference) have not. Unless the whole staff can be oriented and trained to some basic level of understanding, those who have the knowledge and experience will get more and the others will justifiably feel left out. This information-rich, information-poor dichotomy can work against well planned training efforts. If the staff is trained without regard to past experience, those who have experience may intimidate those who have no experience. Even the informal discussion which takes place prior to a staff development activity can have this intimidating effect when some staff members "share" their previous experiences with computers.

The process of involving the library staff in the planning of workstations and local area networking will depend on the planning style of the library management. Some organizations depend on detailed plans with highly structure schedules and carefully defined staff assignments. Other styles depend on a more information "brainstorming" method of planning. Training for all levels of staff about anticipated changes before they occur is essential -- staff deal more effectively with known changes.

Peters issues the following warning (Ref. 7):

> implementation of the new integrated information technology-based systems is much more difficult than anyone dreamed. For one thing, it turns out that the installation of such systems is not primarily a matter of technology. It is a matter of organization. <u>Every</u> power relationship, inside and outside the firm, is affected by the installation of the new information technology systems.
>   (Peter's emphasis)

5. Helping Empower Personnel Through the Change Process

Since staff will react to change, the library administrator can anticipate a number of potential problems and deal with them prior to any equipment choice or installation. Several steps are essential:

    a) demonstrate knowledge of and concern about the work of all the staff
    b) remember the psychological denial processes at work in any social setting.
    c) find out how people really feel about their work situation and about the present equipment and technology they are using.
    d) avoid the tendency to act like systems are fun and easy to use and that people are a problem.
    e) view the development and use of workstations and local area networks as a long term planning and evaluation project involving people as the opportunity arises.

These steps provide a means of empowering the whole library staff, and require some detailed explanation, which follows:

Demonstrate knowledge of and concern about the work of all the staff

The library administrator and his/her staff need to demonstrate that they know the jobs people do and care about the work the rest of the staff is doing. Often the question is: "Does the boss know and care about what I do?" Brod suggests several dimensions of present and future work design that need to be taken into account (Ref. 8):

- knowledge: Are workers' skills being fully used in their present jobs? Is their work sufficiently challenging? Do they want more opportunity to learn new things?
- psychology: Are workers receiving sufficient recognition? Are need for achievement being met? Is there room for advancement?
- efficiency: Is the work exhausting? Is the degree of accuracy required excessive? Is sufficient information provided for maximum job effectiveness?
- task structure: Is there sufficient variety in the work? Are workers given enough scope to use their own initiative? Are they provided with a chance to make planning suggestions?
- ethics: Does management look after the interests of its employees? Do managers convey respect for the skills of the workers? How do workers perceive top management and its goals?

People vary in their ability to process information with any technology (pencil, typewriter, telephone, computer). The employee and his/her immediate supervisor are the best judges of the capabilities in this area. Everyone will not produce the same amount of data (or completed telephone calls). People also vary in their ability to "stick" with a task. Some individuals are not able to monitor their own work pace and need assistance in knowing when to stop and take a break. Some individuals will work a high speed in short bursts...others will be slower but will continue a consistent rate of production over a longer period of time. Institution policy should allow for such variances.

The larger the organization, the more important it is to make public notice of the work of all subordinates on the staff and the contribution that work makes to the overall goals and objectives of the library. The nature of management is that managers not do work, they get others to work. As Hutchins said long ago (Ref. 9):

> The administrator should never do anything he does not have to do, because the things he will have to do are so numerous that he can not possibly have time to do them... He should never do anything he can get anybody to do for him. He should have the largest number of good associates he can find.

The creation of "good associates" at all levels of the library is the basic task of library administration. This empowering of others is essential if the power of technology is to be directed toward good ends. As the planning process for technological change proceeds everyone should be able to identify what their role will be in the emerging structure. When everyone's role and responsibilities are clear, the staff can function more effectively. Part of the staff development process should include a review of the library's history of survived and perhaps even thrived on change. The library administrator needs to be frank about his/her motives in suggesting the change -- what are the "rewards" or benefits which this change will bring about and why are they important to the library?

Often the people who use typewriters, files, telephones have excellent insights as to the usefulness and limitations of these tools. Their ideas about improvements in the work flow and needed equipment capabilities can be helpful in determining what types of workstations and local area networks (if any) are needed. Allowing the staff to participate in planning of workstation and local area network systems, and in assisting with the selection of applications programs and standards, provides a way of enriching the work life of the staff. People can have power. People can acquire information from other individuals working at their peer level in other institutions; people can acquire new and more complex skills; people can make good decisions about what application to use for what purpose; finally, people can be rewarded.

One major reassurance which can be repeatedly stressed is that learning the new systems will take time and that work flow will be slowed during that process. All too often a technology is introduced to "improve work flow performance" which it may do in the longer run, but can not do until people know how to use it and are comfortable with it. Since libraries must remain open specific hours, and continue to serve their clients, library administrators have several options during the training period:

- additional temporary staff to handle some functions while the staff is in training
- discovering staff members who are very proficient at using the system, and temporarily reassigning them as trainers.
- hiring outside organizations to do training for staff members which offers the incentive of academic credit (community college or university) or ease of scheduling.

Remember the denial processes in any social setting.

Facing with the possibility of problems, obstacles, resistance, staff members develop their own denial systems. Denial also influences staff who will deny to themselves and others how they really feel about changes in operations, new equipment, different report forms, etc. Steps can be taken to deal with the denial phenomena: encouraging discussion of the proposed changes, giving illustrations of how people might feel in meetings, and, above all, allowing time for free discussion.

Avoid the tendency to act like systems are fun and easy to use and that people are the problem.

Personal computer systems that work efficiently and allow an information process to develop effectively are exciting. After an individual has worked hard to make a system work...and it does, there is a natural "high." Often these feelings are not shared by the onlookers. When staff members are resistant, seem to refuse to learn new operations, or passively do not take part in planning, the attraction of the efficient machine is very strong. For computer-based technology to work, all of the people with personal computers on their desks must be using the system to communicate and to improve the work process. No library can afford to support two information work process systems: the way we used to do it and the way we are supposed to do it now. The bulk of the administrator's time will be spent helping, encouraging, cajoling staff into moving more and more of their work operations into the computer workstation or local area network environment. Assisting staff in developing the skills and providing the appropriate applications software for their use is the major job of the library administrator.

View the development and use of workstations and local area networks as a long term planning and evaluation project involving people as the opportunity arises.

Since not everyone will enthusiastically support change, the manager can use the planning period prior to installing a computer workstation or local area network system to identify those work groups in the library who are either most interested or most in need of the services such a system can provide. Few organizations will be able to bring their system up "all at once." If the library administrator and staff do a careful analysis of work groups and needs, they will be able to identify areas where current information flow is slowed (or even blocked) as well as areas where the departmental or work group is eager to get involved. Starting with areas of critical need or eagerness, the library director can involve several units in detailed planning, pilot operations, training seminars, etc.

When departments or work groups do a good job utilizing the workstations and the local area network, the library manager needs to be sure that everyone (staff, board of trustees, etc.) knows about how well they are doing. This "island culture" idea has been successfully used in many institutions and is celebrated in Peters and Austin's A Passion for Excellence. (Ref. 10). If the people who are using the system seem to be able to make it work for them in their jobs and seem to be enjoying it, other staff groups may want to get into the act. Many agencies utilize an "electronic newsletter" on the local area network to announce new applications, to praise effective uses, and to share solutions to problems bothering everyone on the system.

The administrator will also need to be aware of what Hannigan calls "the Curve of Nonsatisfaction" as workstation and local area networks continue to be used. This move toward dissatisfaction with the system(s) is usually made up of:

- increased breakdown of hardware
- increased software failures
- increased data loss
- voiced dissatisfaction with software
- reported system slowdowns
- requests for additional and more complex data manipulation and reporting
- suggestions for purchase of peripherals
- increased requests for machine replacement
- requests for newer or enhanced version of software
- reports of frustration because the system does not meet user needs
- breakthrough technology making current architecture obsolete

Since this curve seems inevitable, the administrator must try to anticipate staff concerns and budget requirements for replacement, enhancement, and conversion to newer systems. Information on how the system is working and what particular problems are occurring can provide feedback to long range planning for solutions to problems before they get out of hand.

Part of this long range planning process is the development and announcement of a consistent, humane policy on how the technology of workstation and local area networks is going to be used. The basic principle of policy should be a balance between productivity and worker well-being. The worker's well-being can be enhanced on the job design allows for some type of challenge to be built into workstation and local area network tasks. Work that is too simple breeds boredom and may even cause hostility. Where workers have the opportunity to learn new skills and assume new responsibilities; they have a sense of contributing to the organization as a whole; they are empowered.

Conclusion

Computer-based technology is the process of transforming the way our society handles information and the value of information in our society. Those who can manage information efficiently (quickly) and effectively (to their own ends) will be powerful members of that emerging society. Library administrators have a choice: to be a part of the information society's managers, or to be left behind. Information can not only empower an administrator it can also empower a library system staff and give new energy for that system to create new and successful solutions to the problems facing today's libraries.

REFERENCES

1) Andriole, S. J. The Future of Information Processing Technology. Princeton, NJ: Petrocelli Books, 1985, p. 252.

2) Bland, S. The Media Lab. New York: Viking, 1987.

3) DeBuse, R. (1988). So that's a book...Advancing technology and the library. Information Technology and Libraries 7, No.1, p.7-18, March 1988.

4. The Workstation Revolution. Scientific American 260, No. 5, p. w1-w9, 1989, (Quote is from p. w1).

5. Andriole, op. cit. p .290.

6. Dakshinamurti, G. B. 1985. Automation's Effect on Library Personnel. Canadian Library Journal December p. 343. December 1985. 343-351. (1985, p. 343)

7. Peters, T. J. Thriving on chaos: Handbook for a Management Revolution. Perennial Library Edition. New York: Harper & Row, 1988, (Quote is from p. 637)

8. Brod, C. Technostress: The Human Cost of the Computer Revolution. Menlo Park, CA: Addison-Wesley, 1984. (p. 180ff.)

9. Hutchins, R. M. The Administrator. In Works of the Mind, edited by R. B. Heywood. Chicago: University of Chicago Press, 1947, p. 135-156. (Quote is from p. 138).

10. Peters, T. J. and N. Austin. A Passion for Excellence; The Leadership Difference. New York: Warner Books, 1985..

11. Hannigan, J. A. 1988. An Expanded Managerial Role in a Microcomputer Environment. In Intner, S.S. and Hannigan, J. A. The Library Microcomputer Environment: Management Issues. Phoenix, AZ: Oryx Press, 1988. (list is on page 216).

Titles of Papers Presented at the Meeting for which Text Does Not Appear in the Proceedings

Automating the Reference Statistics: A Multi-User Database Approach
Sanjay R. Chadra, Houston Academy of Medicine—Texas Medical Center Library

System Expansion: Planning for Local Databases
Pat Barkalow Eby, INLEX, Inc.

Selecting an Automated System: Educating Staff and Vendors
Diane Grund and Maria D'Aversa, Moraine Valley Community College

People First, Technology Second: Introducing Your Faculty to Computer Technologies
Elizabeth Patterson, Emory University

Integrated Network Access at the National Agricultural Library
Roberta Y. Rand, National Agricultural Library

Win-Win Negotiation: How to Make the Best Deal with Your Vendor
Joan Frye Williams, INLEX, Inc.

INDEX

This index is based on terms in the titles, added keywords supplied by authors, author's last name, and the author's affiliation.

ALD   39
Arizona State University   83
ARL   149
Assistant Library Director   39
Assistant of Research Libraries   149

Backup media   119
Basista, Thomas   103
BIOETHICSLINE   1
Biomedical Information Resources Center   1
Broering, Naomi C.   1
Brush, Cassandra   11

Card print profiles   11
Case Western Reserve University   97
Casey, Mary H.   19
CD-ROMs   83, 119
Central Missouri State University   131
Chadra, Sanjay R.   169
Chang, S.C.   45
Clink, Kelian D.   25
Collection management   83
Computer Centers management   131
CPU scheduling   19
Crawford, Gregory A.   33
Current Contents   1

Data analysis   11
Database conversion   11
Databases
   electronic   83
   integration   25
Davison, Freida M.   39
Dediu, Horace   45
GTE Laboratories, Inc.   45
DLS MARC UP   53
Document delivery   1, 11
Donahue, Sandra R.   53
Donor-driven systems   145
Drew University   169
DuPage Library System   53
D'Aversa, Maria   169

Eby, Pat Barkalow   169
Educating staff   169
Educating vendors   169
Educational constructs   59
Emory University   169
Engineering   59
ERIC   25
Examination methodology   11
Expert systems   75

Faculty development   169
FAIRS   53
Full test delivery   169

Georgetown University Medical Center Library   1
Graphical user interface   103
Grund, Diane   169

Hardware evaluation   123
Hardware reliability   123
Houston Academy of Medicine Texas Medical Center Library   169
Hurt, C.D.   59
Hypercard   103
Hypermedia   103
HyperRef™   75

IAIMS   1
Indiana University of Pennsylvania   103
Information Access Co.   113
Information access problems   75
Information retrieval   45, 93
Information Systems Consultants, Inc.   19
INLEX, Inc.   169
Institute for Astronomy   141

Jacob, William   65
Jaffe, Lee   73
Jörgensen, Corinne   75
Jörgensen, Peter   75

Knowledge networks   113

Libraries, management 131
Library administration 73, 157
Library automation 113
Library field trials 45
Library systems
  adaptation 93
  selection 93
LIS Electronic Library Systems 1
Local databases 169
Local integrated systems 11
Local location codes 11

Machovec, George S. 83
Management 131
Mankato State University 25
Marc system 53
Medline 25
Mehl, Sharon 93
Memphis State University 123
Metz, Ray E. 97
Micco, Mary 103
Middlebury College 137
Miller, Todd 113
MiniMEDLINE 1
Moraine Valley Community
  College 169
Mori, Martha T. 119
MPE 19
Museum of Science Library 145

National Agriculture Library 169
Natural language mapping 103
Negotiations
  vendor 169
Networking
  Vermont 137
Networks 65, 169
Networks
  cost-effectiveness 137
New England Library
  automation 149
Non-profit institutions 145
Norwalk Public Library 65

Object oriented programming 103
Obsolescence 123
OCLC 53
Online catalogs 73, 149
OPACS 103
Operating systems 19

Paging 19
Patterson, Elizabeth 169
Personnel management 97, 169
PICK 19
Pourciau, Lester J. 123
Project design 11
Public services librarians 33

Rand, Roberta Y. 169
Rao, Dr. Pal V. 131
Reader services 39
Reference automation 75
Reference statistics
  automating 169
Rehbach, Jeffrey 137
Relational database 103
Retrospective conversion 53
Robertson, Kathleen 141
Rockwell International Corp. 119
RTIS/TECHLIB 119
Rutgers University 33

San Francisco State University 39
Scitex Corporation 93
Search strategies 25
Segmentation 19
Selecting automated systems 169
Snyder, Dr. Carol J. 145
Spreadsheets 169
Staff, library 97
Stand-alone systems 65
Statistics 169
St. Francis College 11
Subject access 103
System expansion 169
System migration 65
Systems administrators 33
Systems architecture
  open 65
  proprietary 65

Tebbetts, Diane R. 149
Technical processes 93
Technical services 39
Technocracy 157
Technology 157

University of Arizona 59
University of California 73
University of Hawaii at Manoa 141
University of New Hampshire 149

University of North Carolina at
   Greensboro   157
UNIX evaluation   141
Usage patterns   137

VALS   137
Vermont Automated Library
   System   137
Virtual storage   19
VS   19

Williams, Joan Frye   169
Wright, Keith C.   157

Zappas, Elise T.   169